TROPICAL TREES OF FLORIDA AND THE VIRGIN ISLANDS

A Guide to Identification, Characteristics and Uses

T. Kent Kirk

Pineapple Press, Inc.
Sarasota, Florida

Inquiries should be addressed to:

Pineapple Press, Inc.
P.O. Box 3889
Sarasota, Florida 34230

www.pineapplepress.com

Library of Congress Cataloging-in-Publication Data

Kirk, T. Kent.
  Tropical trees of Florida and the Virgin Islands : a guide to identification, characteristics and uses / T. Kent Kirk. -- 1st ed.
      p. cm.
  Includes bibliographical references and index.
  ISBN 978-1-56164-445-2 (pb : alk. paper)
  1. Trees--Florida--Identification. 2. Trees--Virgin Islands--Identification. 3. Tropical plants--Florida--Identification. 4. Tropical plants--Virgin Islands--Identification. I. Title.
  QK154.K57 2009
  582.1609759--dc22
                        2008043345

First Edition
10 9 8 7 6 5 4 3 2 1

Design by Karen Nelson
Printed in China

CONTENTS

Preface

The quality and number of commonly available books on the flora of the Virgin Islands have increased considerably in recent years, possibly as a result of spreading interest in the environment, or a growing concern about the future of the native forest. Both these reasons have sent residents and tourists alike in search of something more than "pretty pictures of trees."

The several islands that together make up the U.S. and British Virgin Islands are fortunate to have a number of botanical works dating back to the seventeenth century, which together give a fairly continuous view of the life and uses of the area. Unfortunately, these books are mostly held in libraries, museums, or research departments and are not available to the casual enquirer. For this reason we will be glad to have Kent Kirk's *Tropical Trees of Florida and the Virgin Islands,* a book based on years of work for the U.S. Forest Service and the University of Wisconsin, combined with a deep appreciation for the trees he describes. This book is not a formal flora, but a more relaxed though accurate and thorough description of some of the outstanding trees in the area, their habits of growth and their local uses. It includes a large number of color photographs. The book contains a large percentage of native trees, but also many of the "exotics" that have been introduced over hundreds of years of human occupancy.

We hope that the information will prove sufficiently interesting to encourage some readers to try to cultivate the more desirable of these trees, as many of the native trees are in danger of elimination as a result of development.

Margaret Hayes
Herbarium Curator
St. George Village Botanical Garden
St. Croix, U.S. Virgin Islands

ACKNOWLEDGMENTS

Preparing this book would have been very difficult if not impossible without the generous help of others, to whom I offer my gratitude and thanks. Foremost are those at the St. George Village Botanical Garden on St. Croix, especially Herbarium Curator (and former nursery owner and horticulturalist) Margaret Hayes (who wrote the preface to this book), and Chief Horticulturist David Hamada. Also on St. Croix, Jozef (Jeff) Keularts, Extension Specialist at the University of the Virgin Islands, was most helpful and generous with his time. Jeff also made some of the photographs, as noted. Margaret Hayes and Jeff Keularts reviewed the manuscript for technical accuracy, an invaluable service. On St. Thomas, Toni Thomas, Extension Agent and author at the University of the Virgin Islands; and on St. John, naturalist and author Eleanor Gibney, were most helpful and generous in helping me locate and identify trees. All of these experts not only helped me locate trees, but also advised me on which trees to include. Margaret Hayes, David Hamada, Toni Thomas, and Eleanor Gibney completed surveys for each of the Virgin Islands as to how common the various trees are. Prof. Emeritus Daniel B. Ward of the University of Florida kindly told me which of the V.I. trees are also found in south Florida, and Roger L. Hammer, naturalist and author in Homestead, Florida, told me how common each is in south Florida and answered many questions about the trees as they occur there. Several others helped me locate trees, including Aberra Bulbulla of the Agricultural Experiment Station, U.S.V.I., St. Croix; Errol Chichester of the Department of Agriculture, U.S.V.I., St. Croix; Rudy O'Reilly, Jr., U.S.D.A. Natural Resources Conservation Service, St. Croix; Oriel Smith of Caneel Bay resort, St. John; and Irene Lawaetz of the Lawaetz Plantation, St. Croix. Several friends helped me in my search for trees and in photographing them, including Joyce Hilgers, Vickie and Greg Zeikus, Mary Dominski, and Dale Morton, Extension Specialist at the University of the Virgin Islands, who kindly provided two photos. Finally, I want to single out my old friend Tom Miller, who spent many hours critiquing and discussing all aspects of the book. He also helped me in locating trees and taking some of the photographs, as noted. As he explains in the Foreword, Tom and I started this project together, but he had to drop out because of illness.

I also want to thank the following hotels and resorts for allowing me to photograph trees on their grounds: Caneel Bay resort, St. John; The Westin, St. John; The Ritz Carlton, St. Thomas; and The Buccaneer, St. Croix.

Finally, I want to recognize John Lorimer for advice on digital photography, Karen Nelson for the design and layout of the book, and June Cussen and Helena Berg for editing the text.

FOREWORD

This book probably had its origin 45 years ago when Kent and I began our graduate degrees in plant pathology at North Carolina State University. During the six or seven years we were at N.C. State, Kent and I became close friends. After earning our Ph.D.s, both of us were employed by the U.S.D.A. Forest Service as research scientists, Kent at the Forest Products Laboratory on the campus of the University of Wisconsin, and I at the Forestry Sciences Laboratory at the University of Georgia, and later at the Forestry Sciences Laboratory at Olustee, Florida. I also had a joint appointment at the University of Florida, and Kent at the University of Wisconsin. Although Kent and I stayed in contact over the next 30 years, we rarely met.

In the mid-1990s personal tragedies brought us together again: both our wives died. Since we were both retired by this time, we began exchanging visits and engaging in our favorite hobbies—fishing, cooking, woodworking, and spending time in the woods, where we spent many enjoyable hours arguing about the identity of trees we encountered.

For over twenty years, Kent and his wife had spent winter vacations in the Caribbean Islands, and fell in love with them, and Kent continued after she died. In 2002, Kent invited me to join him on St. John in the U.S. Virgin Islands. The trees intrigued us, and we set out to find a book or books to help us get to know them. This was frustrating, because we could not find an adequate book for the islands, and were unable to identify more than a handful of species. At this point, we started discussing doing a book ourselves that people could use without having an advanced degree in botany. We started our initial effort in the Miami area and in the Florida Keys. Our next trip was to the island of St. Croix, with its impressive St. George Village Botanical Garden. Shortly after returning from St. Croix, I became ill and was forced to withdraw from involvement with the book.

Kent decided to continue, and with great determination has produced a worthy product. The writing, photography, and travel necessary to write this book required a monumental effort on Kent's part, including consultations with highly knowledgeable people in both the V.I. and Florida. I have enjoyed helping him from time to time.

This book should be of great value to anyone with an interest in the trees of the V.I. and south Florida, especially those who wish to identify trees without a great deal of technical botanical knowledge. Tourists visiting the two locations, as well as permanent residents, can identify and learn something about the many beautiful trees growing in these tropical areas since this book is both technically accurate and entertaining to read.

Thomas Miller
Retired, U.S. Forest Service
Courtesy Professor, University of Florida

INTRODUCTION

The beauty and diversity of the tropical trees in the Virgin Islands (V.I.) and south Florida are apparent to thousands of visitors every year and appreciated by those who live there, many of whom are avid gardeners. To those like the author interested in learning more about them—their identities, characteristics, and uses—the absence of a fairly comprehensive, user-friendly field guide to both native and introduced species in the V.I. has been frustrating. This prompted my friend Tom Miller and me, in 2002, to look into preparing such a guide, and that led, six years later, to this book. I hope it will satisfy those curious about the trees.

I designed the book to be as nontechnical as possible and to be easy to use by virtue of its organization, layout, and numerous color photographs.

Each tree species is illustrated with photos of the tree as a whole, its bark, leaves, flowers, fruit, and in some cases, special structures. Sizes are included as scale bars or in captions. The text for each tree includes the following: an introduction giving the key identifying features of the species, whether it is native or introduced, and how common it is. This is followed by descriptions of the form; the leaves and bark; the flowers; the fruit; favored habitat, including drought-, wind-, and salt-tolerance; and uses. Endangered species are noted, as are those that have become weedy. Most of my information is taken from the sources cited at the end of the book (p.205), as well as from personal observations.

Almost all of the trees have been used in folk medicines, so this information is included under "uses." It is interesting to speculate about how those medical uses were determined; it must have been painful in many cases! The information about medical uses is mainly from the Internet, primarily from universities and government organizations. The author does not advocate trying any of the folk medical uses! Ayensu summarized West Indian uses of medicinal plants in 1981; his book contains over half of the trees included here. More recently, Thomas (1997) described medicinal uses of plants in the U.S. Virgin Islands, and her book, too, includes several of this book's species. Beginning in earnest more than 30 years ago, extensive scientific research has been done on medicinal plants, including most of the trees here, resulting in a huge literature. The interested reader thus has many resources for pursuing the folk medicine claims.

The names of the trees are given four ways: the Latin (scientific) name, with authority; common English name or names; one or more Spanish common name(s); and a French common name. The Latin, Spanish, and French names are italicized. Most of the trees, if not all, have many—often dozens—of common or local names, but I have made no attempt to be comprehensive. (The books by Little *et al.* list many of them.) Too, several different tree species often have the same common name (thus the importance of scientific names).

THE TROPICS AND TROPICAL TREES

The Tropics are defined as the band around the earth between latitudes of 23.5° north and 23.5° south of the equator. In this band, the sun is always high in the sky and seasonal variation is relatively minor. The V.I. lie within this band, but south Florida does not. Even so, south Florida's climate is such that over 90% of the V.I. trees in this book are found in both places. We define south Florida as the Keys and the southernmost area of the peninsula.

The V.I. lie between 17° and 19° north of the equator, with the Caribbean Sea to the south and the Atlantic Ocean to the north. They are at the western end of the Lesser Antilles. Their geological origin is both volcanic and tectonic (causing the uplifting of the ocean floor), giving them a variety of soil types. This diversity of soils, coupled with their tropical location and fairly high hills, provides the V.I. with a rich range of ecosystems. The larger islands of the Caribbean, comprising the Greater Antilles—Puerto Rico, Jamaica, Cuba and Hispaniola— have a much greater diversity of climates, elevations, soil types, and ecosystems, resulting in an almost bewildering number of tree species. Once part of the Puerto Rican land mass (with the exception of St. Croix), the V.I. share their tree species with modern-day Puerto Rico (as does St. Croix). However, as mentioned, Puerto Rico has more ecosystems and, consequently, many more species of trees.

South Florida has much in common with the V.I., but there are important differences as well. The soils of south Florida are not of volcanic origin, rather are derived from limestone (sea sediments), or are primarily sand. Through the ages, too, they have accumulated a rich organic layer in some places. The major difference for our purposes is that both tropical and temperate zone trees grow in south Florida. Only a few of the trees in this book have ranges that extend significantly into the temperate zone. The temperate zone species in south Florida do not occur in the V.I.

The tropical trees of the V.I. and south Florida are of two origins: native and introduced (exotics). Many of the introduced ones have escaped cultivation, and it is difficult now to know whether some are native or were introduced—especially those native to other Caribbean Islands or other parts of the tropical Americas. With the help of the experts acknowledged above, and the literature, I have noted which trees are native and which not, and in the uncertain cases, have made a note of that as well. To my knowledge, none of the trees included here is endemic to the V.I. or south Florida—i.e. found only there originally.

Most of the more than 90 species of trees included here are found on all of the Virgin Islands and in south Florida. They do vary in their frequency of occurrence, however. With the help of the experts acknowledged above, I have included that information about the various species.

The book's few trees that occur in the V.I. but not south Florida are these: *Caesalpinia coriaria* (dividivi), *Calophyllum antillanum* (galba, found in Fairchild Tropical Botanic Garden in Coral Gables), *Cordia rickseckeri* (orange manjack), *Guapira fragrans* (black mampoo), *Myrciaria floribunda* (guavaberry, in Fairchild Garden), *Consolea rubescens* (tree cactus), *Pilosocereus royenii* (pipe-organ cactus, in Fairchild Garden), *Pimenta racemosa* (bay-rum-tree, in Fairchild Garden), *Piscidia carthagenensis* (fishpoison-tree), and *Zanthoxylum martinicense* (white-prickle).

In south Florida, the reader might become interested in trees that are not in this book. They are not included in part because many are temperate zone species; examples include several *Quercus* spp. (oaks), *Taxodium distichum* (baldcypress), *Pinus* spp. (pines), and *Diospyros virginiana* (common persimmon). They do not occur in the V.I. Other woody plants are not included because they do not reach tree size by my definition. But according to Little (1978) and Nelson (1994) (see citation list p. 205), south Florida has some true tropical trees that are not found in the V.I. These are not included in this book except where mentioned in descriptions of closely related V.I. species. Several Florida tropical species are considered rare, and several more are limited to very small areas, so are unlikely to be encountered and are not included here. In any case, Nelson describes most of the missing trees, making his book a good source of additional information for south Florida trees. Roger Hammer's *Florida Keys Wildflowers* (Falcon Press, 2004) is also useful for some of these trees, especially if flowers are present. These books do not include most of the species in my book. The Florida tropical trees that are not mentioned in my book include these: *Amphitecna latifolia* (black calabash; also in the V.I. but uncommon), *Citharexylum spinosum* (fiddlewood; can be found on St. Croix and St. Thomas), *Drypetes laterifolia* (Guiana-plum, Keys only), *Exothea paniculata* (inkwood), *Gymnanthes lucida* (oysterwood; also in the V.I. but uncommon), *Manilkara jaimiqui* (wild dilly, Keys only), *Mastichodendron foetidissimum* (false-mastic; can be found in the V.I.), *Metopium toxiferum* (poisonwood), *Simarouba glauca* (paradise-tree), *Thrinax radiata* (Florida thatch palm, Keys), and *Zanthoxylum fagara* (wild lime).

How to Use This Book

Note: a brief glossary is found on p. 204. The terms defined there will be familiar to most readers, but it might be a good idea to refresh your memory.

Because leaves are almost always present on the trees of the V.I. and south Florida, I have organized the trees primarily according to leaf type. Palms and cactuses, easily recognized as such, are treated separately in their own sections. Also, a few of the trees are so unusual and/or noticeable that I have separated them out in a first section. It is probably a good idea to thumb through that first section to start with to see what I mean by "unusual and/or noticeable," and to see which trees are included.

To identify the tree of interest, the reader should do the following:

1. If the tree is a palm or cactus, go to those sections and identify it from the photos and descriptions.

2. If the tree is not a palm or cactus, decide if it looks unusual and/or noticeable to you. If it does, go back to the photos in the first section and see if there is a match. For example, when you first look at a papaya tree, it will look unusual to you.

3. If the tree does not look unusual or odd to you, then decide what type of leaves it has using the photo examples here, then page to the appropriate section of the book. First, determine whether the leaves are simple or compound.

Simple leaves arise singly from the twig (or, in some cases, from the trunk or branches). Simple leaves can be alternate (leaves not in pairs, but alternating along the twig), or opposite (pairs of leaves arising directly opposite each other on the twig).

Compound leaves either have multiple leaflets arising from a single point at the end of the petiole, or along a midrib. If the leaflets arise from the end of the petiole rather than along a midrib, they are termed

Simple, alternate (p. 30)

Annona squamosa (sugar-apple)

Simple, opposite (p. 88)

Pimenta racemosa (bay-rum-tree)

palmately compound. If the leaflets occur along a midrib, they are said to be pinnately compound. Pinnate leaves can be twice pinnate (termed bipinnately compound), or even thrice pinnate (termed tripinnately compound). Note that compound leaves can also be alternate or opposite with respect to how the petioles are attached to the twig.

These six leaf types are illustrated here. I strongly suggest that the user thumb through sections to see the variation in leaves within a section.

Some leaves can fool you. Several trees, for example *Crescentia cujete* (calabash-tree), have simple leaves that are so clustered that it is difficult to determine if they are opposite or alternate. In fact, in this book, all clustered leaves are alternate except those of *Randia aculeata* (box-briar).

Also, in very dry years, some trees lose their leaves—and a few trees lose them every winter; in these cases, you can often find fallen leaves under the tree—or other individuals of the same species in the area that have not yet lost all their leaves, or will lose them at a different time. Trees are not as synchronized in tropical climates as they are in climates where seasonal changes are greater, so you will sometimes find a leafless individual of a species standing next to one that has leaves. When leaves cannot be found, other features will have to be used, such as flowers or persisting seed pods, together with the photos.

4. When all else fails, just thumb through the book until you see your tree.

In the V.I., the trees you find should be in the book, with a few exceptions. Those exceptions are because they are not very noticeable or are uncommon: rare natives, or exotics planted only as curiosities or ornamentals. In south Florida, as mentioned above, some of the trees you see will not be in the book, for the same reasons as in the V.I., or they might be temperate zone species, deliberately not included here.

I wish you success and pleasure as you get to know these trees!

T. Kent Kirk

Compound, pinnate (p. 118)

Andira inermis (angelin)

Compound, bipinnate (p. 152)

Peltophorum pterocarpum (yellow flamboyant)

Compound, tripinnate (p.172)

Moringa oleifera (horseradish-tree)

Compound, palmate (p. 176)

Adansonia digitata (baobab)

Easily recognized species

Several of the trees in this book are odd and/or unusual, and will be remembered once identified. The reader will recognize most of them as being different from most others encountered. Some of them, too, including *Araucaria heterophylla* (Norfolk-Island-pine), *Casuarina equisetifolia* (casuarina) and *Parkinsonia aculeata* (Jerusalem-thorn) do not fit well into the leaf type categories. For these reasons, eight species have been included in this first, separate section on "Easily Identified Species."

Carica papaya (papaya)

Ravenala madagascariensis (travelers-tree)

Araucaria heterophylla (Salisb.) Franco

Norfolk-Island-pine, *araucaria, arbre de fer*

Araucariaceae

This tree, at St. George Village Botanical Garden on St. Croix in November, was about 60 ft. (18 m) tall and 15 in. (38 cm) in dbh.

Norfolk-Island-pine is one of the best known and most easily recognized trees in the V.I. and south Florida. It is an attractive tree, recognized by its: (1) distinct form, usually with a single straight trunk; (2) whorls of nearly horizontal branches; and (3) slender twigs arranged in a horizontal plane and covered with small dark green leaves. A native of tiny Norfolk Island in the South Pacific, it has been planted in tropical areas around the world for its beauty and is grown widely as a house plant. This striking tree is readily located on all of the major Virgin Islands and in south Florida, although it is not particularly abundant.

Form. The whorls of 4–7 horizontal branches have many slender ropelike twigs arranged in "Vs". In the V.I. and south Florida, the tree seldom exceeds 75 ft. (23 m) in height and 24 in. (61 cm) in trunk diameter. However, in environments similar to that of its native habitat it can reach 200 ft. (61 m) tall and over 36 in. (91 cm) in diameter.

View showing a branch.

Leaves. The alternate, needlelike leaves are of two types. Young ones are 0.25–0.5 in. (0.6–1.3 cm) long, occurring in spirals around the twigs. Older leaves are broader, small, scalelike needles and are crowded around the twigs. Twigs with attached leaves fall together when several years old.

Flowers. The inconspicuous flowers appear in the spring.

Juvenile (above) and adult leaves.

Fruits. Norfolk-Island-pine is a conifer (cone-bearing gymnosperm). It rarely reproduces in the V.I. or Florida. Where it does reproduce it has male cones that are oblong, 1.5–2 in. (3.8–5 cm) long, and, on separate trees, female cones that are more rounded and longer (4–5 in., 10–13 cm). Cones are green. Seeds are triangular and winged, about 1.25 in. (3.2 cm) on a side and flat.

Habitat. *Araucaria heterophylla* is a hardy plant, growing in a variety of soil types. It is tolerant of salt and is planted near beaches. It also has high drought-tolerance, but is not resistant to high wind.

Uses. Norfolk-Island-pine is used mainly as a houseplant, being common in the U.S. and Europe. In the tropics, it is a stunning horticultural tree, with its eye-catching foliage and symmetrical form. However, it can become quite tall, dwarfing nearby dwellings and other trees. The wood is soft and resinous. Wood of particularly large specimens, probably free of knots, was used on its native Norfolk Island for boatbuilding and other construction. The wood of smaller trees is suitable for any use for which weak and soft wood suffices. In Hawaii, the wood is a favorite for making turned objects because the knots produce interesting patterns. No reference to medicinal uses was found.

Artocarpus altilis (Parkinson) Fosberg

breadfruit, *panapén, pana de pepitas, chataignier*

Moraceae (mulberry family)

Open-grown wide-spreading tree with multiple stems arising near the base. The tree, photographed in Queens Quarter, St. Croix, in May, was approximately 50 ft. tall and 36 in. in diameter near the ground (15 m, 91 cm).

Brought into the West Indies in 1793 by the infamous Captain Bligh of *Mutiny on the Bounty* fame, breadfruit is one of the most important foods in the tropics worldwide. It is easily recognized by its: (1) large, lobed, shiny green leaves; (2) big, round green fruits; (3) milky juice that exudes from cut bark; and (4) large, fleshy, tight yellow masses of tiny flowers. Flowers and fruits are found all year. Breadfruit is native to the South Pacific islands. Its distinctive appearance makes it easy to spot (usually in yards), but it is not especially common in the V.I. or south Florida.

Form. Breadfruit trees get to be about 60 ft. (18 m) tall in the V.I. and south Florida. usually with a single trunk to 24 in. (61 cm) in diameter and a wide, spreading crown. Trees half again as large are found in some tropical areas. Branches are of two types: long ones with leaves clustered near the ends, and shorter ones with lateral leaf-bearing twigs.

Leaves and bark. Leaves are simple and alternate, arranged in a spiral pattern on the branches. They have short stout petioles and are 9–25 in. (23–64 cm) long and 8–20 in. (20–51 cm) wide, with 7–11 deep lobes. The bark is relatively smooth, and has numerous small lenticels.

Flowers. Male and female flowers are born separately on the same tree. They are very numerous and tiny, aggregated into elongated masses on stalks that are about 2 in. (5 cm) long. Male aggregates are about 1 in. (2.5 cm) in diameter and 5–12 in. (13–30 cm) long, yellowish, turning brown and falling off. Female aggregates are light green and about 1.5 in. (3.8 cm) in diameter and 2.5 in. (6.4 cm) long.

Fruits are large, 4–8 in. (10–20 cm) long, usually round but sometimes elliptical. They are actually aggregates of individual fruits, delineated on the surface by small 4- to 6-sided irregular faces, each with a conical spine in the seeded varieties. The white starchy pulp becomes creamy at maturity, and does not have much flavor. Large brown seeds, when present (several per fruit), are edible.

Habitat. Breadfruit trees are strictly tropical, preferring hot humid conditions and plenty of water and sun. They thrive on deep fertile, well-drained soils. They are not drought-tolerant, but are somewhat tolerant of salt. It is unlikely that they are very wind-tolerant because of the large leaves and dense crowns.

Leaves were about 24 in. (61 cm) long and the fruit 6 in. (15 cm) in diameter; photographed in November.

Male flower cluster, approximately 7 in. (18 cm) long.

Emerging fruit.

Uses. Many varieties of breadfruit are grown in orchards. The fruit is prepared and eaten when immature in much the same way as potatoes, whereas the fully ripe, sweeter fruit is cooked and eaten as a fruit. The fruit of most varieties is purgative if eaten raw. Seeds are boiled or roasted and eaten like chestnuts. Bark fiber has been used to make textiles, rope, and other products. The wood is very lightweight, little used in furniture or construction. However, the wood is surprisingly strong and has been used to make surfboards and bongo drum carcasses in Hawaii. Several medical uses for the leaves and latex have been reported; for example, a decoction of the leaves is said to lower blood pressure and relieve asthma, and the diluted latex is used to treat diarrhea. Cooked fruit has been used to relieve constipation.

Carica papaya L.

papaya, *lechosa, papayo, papayer*

Caricaceae

An isolated specimen on the east end of St. John; this tree was approximately 20 ft. (6 m) tall and had a dbh of 7 in. (18 cm). Inset shows bark dappled with light.

Papaya fruits are well known to all, being widely available in grocery stores and markets in most parts of the world. The evergreen tree is odd-looking and easily identified by its (1) upright form with large, multi-lobed leaves clustered at the top of the trunk; (2) the familiar fruits in various stages of maturity clustered under the leaves; and (3) pale yellow flowers. Some trees bear only male flowers, so do not have fruit. Papaya has flowers and/or fruit year-round. The origin of papaya is not known with certainty, but some think it came from southern Mexico. It has now been planted throughout the world's tropics, and is common on all the major Virgin Islands and south Florida.

Form. Papaya attains a height of 20 ft. (6 m) or more, and the trunk usually is 8 in. (20 cm) or less in diameter. The crown is rounded, 6–10 ft. (2–3 m) in diameter. It is single-stemmed at the base, and usually to the top, but some trees have secondary stems (probably the result of injury); these curve up and grow parallel to the main one.

Leaves and bark. Leaves are deeply seven- to nine-lobed, and the lobes are divided again. They are up to 2.5 ft. (0.8 m) across, with hollow petioles 1–3 ft. (0.3–0.9 m) or more long. Leaves are dull light green above and pale whitish-green below, although some varieties have purple leaves. Bark is smooth, with thin horizontal leaf scar lines.

This leaf, photographed in May, was about 20 in. (51 cm) across.

Flowers. Male and female flowers may occur on different plants, or flowers may be bisexual. Female and bisexual flowers are about 2 in. (5 cm) long, nearly stalkless, and borne singly or in small groups at the leaf bases. Male flowers occur in branched clusters up to 2 ft. (60 cm) long. Individual male flowers are 1–1.5 in. (2.5–4 cm) long; the tubular structures open to reveal five slender petals and a yellow center.

Interior of the crown of a male tree showing abundant flowers and unopened buds; insets show female flower and young fruit (top, February), and male flower (bottom, November).

Fruits. In the V.I. and south Florida, one most commonly encounters papaya fruits that are oblong, 6–15 in. (15–38 cm) long and 4–6 in. (10–15 cm) in diameter. When mature, the soft orange flesh is sweet and tasty. Fruit centers are hollow, with round black seeds.

Habitat. Papaya is more fastidious than many of its associates. It needs adequate rainfall, well-drained soils—slightly acidic to neutral—and it is easily damaged by strong winds. It is not salt-tolerant.

Uses. *Carica papaya* is widely grown locally or (in south Florida and elsewhere) in orchards. Papaya is plagued by many diseases and insects, which modern biotechnology research and breeding are addressing. A latex obtained from the immature fruit, also found in the leaves and stems, contains two protein-digesting enzymes, papain and chymopapain. These are used as meat tenderizers and beer clarifiers, and for many other purposes. Extracts of various plant parts have been used widely in folk medicines. Uses include as an abortifacient and as treatments for rheumatism, asthma, chest colds, diarrhea, arthritis, boils, worm infections, warts, skin fungi, and even cancers. Unripe papaya fruit is cooked as a vegetable, as are young leaves in some countries.

Crown of an orchard tree on St. Croix in May; fruit turning yellow was about 10 in. (25 cm) long.

Casuarina equisetifolia L.

casuarina, weeping-willow, Australian-pine, beefwood, she-oak, horsetail casuarina, *ciprés, pino de Australia, pin de l'Australie*

Casuarinaceae (casuarina family)

This rather typical specimen, photographed in February on the grounds of the Buccaneer Hotel, St. Croix, was 14 in. (36 cm) in diameter near its base, and about 70 ft. (21 m) tall.

Once seen, casuarina is a tree that will be easily recognized in future encounters. It looks like a pine, but is not related. It is recognized by its (1) tall slender form with long willowy branches; (2) feathery, drooping, pale light green twigs that look like pine needles; and (3) small pine cone–like fruits. Casuarina is an import from northern Australia and surrounding areas, has been planted widely in tropical locales, and is common in the V.I. and south Florida. In many areas, including south Florida, it escapes and is considered a serious invader. It hasn't spread in Puerto Rico because ants eat the seeds, which perhaps is true in the V.I. as well, because it does not seem to be invasive there either. Its graceful foliage, ever rustling gently in the trade winds, is a pleasure to eye and ear.

Form. Usually having a single trunk, casuarina has long limbs that angle upward, then arc over under the weight of their many "needles" and fruits. The crown is open. The tree can attain a height of 150 ft. (46 m) and a trunk diameter of over 18 in. (46 cm) but is smaller in the V.I. and south Florida.

Leaves. The "leaves" or "needles" of casuarina are not actually leaves. Instead, the long, thin green twigs have rings of minute (0.03 in., 0.8 mm long) grayish, real leaves about every 0.25 in. (0.6 cm). The twigs are shed periodically like leaves, but the tree is evergreen.

Flowers. Male and female flowers are separate, but occur on the same tree. The former are elongated, club-shaped clusters about 0.12 in. (0.3 cm) in diameter, and 0.5 in. (1.3 cm) long at twig ends, whereas the females are in short-stalked lateral spherical clusters about 0.25 in. (0.6 cm) in diameter. The pale yellowish to red flowers are found year-round.

Fruits are green knobby clusters (about 0.5 in., 1.3 cm in diameter) of tiny angular "balls" with points. When mature they turn brown and each ball splits open in two halves to release a single seed. The seeds are winged, about 0.25 in. (0.6 cm) long. Dispersal is by wind, water, and birds. Fruits in various stages of maturity are found year-round.

Habitat. Casuarina is a robust tree, resisting most conditions except shade, high winds, and prolonged inundation. Bacterial associates of its roots fix atmospheric nitrogen, so it survives on very poor soils, which it actually improves. The tree is very salt- and drought-tolerant, and can survive periodic flooding for short periods. It is usually found in coastal areas growing on sandy sites.

Uses. Casuarina wood, heavy and very hard, has ruined many a saw blade. Once cut and dried, however, it is a valued and excellent firewood, perhaps its main use in many parts of the world. The wood has been used in a number of ways, but its seasoning and woodworking difficulties, and dimensional instability, make it a challenge. The bark has been used in folk medicines as an astringent, diuretic, and laxative, and for treatment of beri-beri, cough, and many other problems. Tannin from the bark has been used to tan hides. The tree grows very rapidly and has been used as a soil stabilizer and windbreak (although its shallow root system makes it prone to being blown over in strong winds). In the V.I. it is planted as an ornamental.

The thin, green twigs resemble pine needles; the longest here were about 8 in. (20 cm).

December photograph showing female flowers among the twigs; inset shows a male flower at a twig end. Female flowers were 0.4 in. (1 cm) long, and the male flower 0.1 in. (0.25 cm) long.

Mature fruit cones on limb, some open; they were about 0.5 in. (1.3 cm) in diameter. Inset shows open cone and seed, about 0.1 in. (0.25 cm) long. Photographs taken in February.

Parkinsonia aculeata L.

Jerusalem-thorn, horse-bean, *palo de rayo, arête-boeuf*

Fabaceae (pea family)

Tree approximately 20 ft. (6 m) tall and 6 in. (15 cm) in diameter at the base, photographed at South Gate, St. Croix, in March.

Jerusalem-thorn is an unusual tree, native to the dry southwestern U.S., Mexico, and probably farther south, where it is often found growing with mesquite. It is identified by its (1) long, thin, evergreen leaves, many with tiny leaflets, which are later shed; (2) green or yellow-green branches and twigs; (3) beautiful yellow flowers; and (4) thorns on the twigs and branches. Flowers and fruits are present all year in the V.I., and in the summer in south Florida. Jerusalem-thorn has been planted widely for its showy flowers in the West Indies, where it has become naturalized. It has also become naturalized, following planting, all across the southernmost U.S., from south Florida to California. The species is readily found but not especially common in the U.S. Virgin Islands, but more common on the major British Virgin Islands.

Form. Jerusalem-thorn is a small tree up to 25 ft. (7.6 m) in height, and perhaps 8 in. (20 cm) in trunk diameter. It has an open, airy, spreading crown to 20 ft. (6 m) in diameter. It often, if not usually, branches near the ground. Branches are slender and often droop.

Leaves with tiny leaflets, and thorns. Longest leaf was about 12 in. (30 cm) long.

Leaves and bark. The alternate leaves are actually bipinnately compound, though that is not obvious. Each consists of a thorn midrib and 1 or 2 pairs of drooping yellow-green leaves bearing 20–30 pairs of tiny (about 0.25 in., 0.6 cm long) leaflets. The 8–16 in. (20–41 cm)–long ribbonlike midribs persist and, together with the green twigs and branches, carry out photosynthesis. In addition to the leaf thorn, the twig nodes bear pairs of thorns up to 1 in. (2.5 cm) long.

Flowers occur in lateral branched clusters 3–8 in. (7.5–20 cm) long, opening from the base up. Individual flowers are about 0.75 in. (2 cm) across, with five separate petals and showy red centers.

Flowers were about 0.75 in. (2 cm) across; photographed in February on St. Thomas.

Fruits. Clusters of fruit pods, green becoming yellowish-brown, are 3–4 in. (7.5–10 cm) long, pointed, and constricted between the seeds. Seeds are brown, about 0.5 in. (1.3 cm) long.

Habitat. Jerusalem-thorn is a desert plant and very drought-resistant. It tolerates a variety of soil types, as well as salinity. It is probably wind-resistant by virtue of its thin crown and small size.

Uses. Used mainly as an ornamental, *P. aculeata* is also planted as living fence posts and hedges, and to stabilize desert soils and sand. In some areas (Australia, Hawaii), the plant is considered to be a serious invasive species. Ornamental use is declining for this reason, as well as because the tree is host to many problems and is difficult to handle horticulturally. Bacteria associated with the tree roots fix atmospheric nitrogen, thus enriching the soil. The sapwood is yellowish and thick, the heartwood brown. The wood is moderately heavy and hard, but used only locally, for fuel. Infusions of leaves, fruit, flowers, and bark have been used in home remedies to treat arthritis, rheumatism, fever, malaria, and as a stimulant and abortive agent. Livestock graze on the leaves, and in the U.S. desert southwest, Indians once gathered, roasted, and ate the seeds.

Nearly mature and mature pods with seed, photographed in May on St. Croix.

Plumeria alba L.

white frangipani, milktree, milky bush, nosegaytree, *alelí, frangipanier sauvage*

Apocynaceae (dogbane family)

This large white frangipani tree near Five Corners on St. Croix in May was 12 in. (30 cm) in trunk diameter at the base and approximately 18 ft. (5.5 m) tall. Black patches on the bark might reflect exposure to fire.

White frangipani is an unusual looking tree because it has stout, sparse limbs terminated by clusters of leaves. This evergreen tree is recognized by its (1) sparse, stubby branches; (2) stiff, narrow, simple leaves, which are alternate, with prominent veins; (3) beautiful, very fragrant white flowers; (4) pairs of prominent seed pods; and (5) milky sap released by wounding the bark (hence the reference to milk in some names). Flowers are seen almost year-round, and fruit for much of the year. The tree is native to the V.I. and surrounding islands, and is used as an ornamental in south Florida. A similar, related tree, *Plumeria rubra*, native to Central America, has been planted more commonly as an ornamental, because of its larger flowers that may be white, but are usually red-toned.

Form. Frequently, white frangipani has multiple stems arising near the ground, but can have a single trunk. It becomes 25–30 ft. (7.6–9 m) tall with trunk diameters to 8 in. (20 cm) or larger. The crown is spreading but thin because of the relatively few branches.

Leaves and bark. Leaf blades are stiff, 6–15 in. (15–38 cm) long, thick, dark green on top and almost white on bottom, with smooth turned-down margins. Veins are nearly at right angles to the midrib. Interestingly, many trees are completely denuded by the caterpillar *Pseudosphinx tetrio* in late winter. The fairly smooth bark is gray-brown.

Leaves and a flower, photographed in May on St. John; longest leaves were about 12 in. (30 cm). Inset shows the caterpillar that denudes many trees, in February on St. John; these were about 3 in. (7.6 cm) long.

Flowers are in clusters on stalks 3–8 in. (7.6–20 cm) long. Individual flowers are on short stalks, and are 1.5–2 in. (4–5 cm) long and broad. They contain both male and female organs.

Fruit pods are in pairs, green becoming brown when mature. They are 4–6 in. (10–15 cm) long and about 0.5 in. (1.3 cm) in diameter. Each contains numerous winged seeds.

Habitat. *Plumeria alba* is part of the dry thorn woodland ecosystem of the V.I. (though it has no thorns). It is very drought-resistant, does well in a variety of soil types, is moderately salt-tolerant, and is wind-resistant.

Individual flowers were about 2 in. (5 cm) across. Photographed in February on St. John.

Uses. The main use of *Plumeria* is as an ornamental. The wood of white frangipani is hard, heavy, and tough, and, when

Plumeria rubra can have red or white flowers; note that the leaves are wider than those of *P. alba*. Photo taken in February on St. John.

the tree is large enough, it finds occasional uses in carpentry. Extracts of the bark have been used in folk medicines for treatment of warts, gonorrhea, and as a purgative, and the latex to treat wounds, skin parasites, toothache, and even syphilis. Essential oil from the blossoms is commercially produced for use in perfumes and aromatherapy products. In Hawaii, *Plumerias* are grown in orchards for their blossoms, used to make the famous leis.

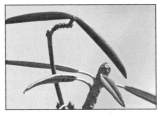

Mature and immature fruit pods, 4–6 in. (10–15 cm) long, in February on St. John.

Ravenala madagascariensis Sonn.

travelers-tree, travelers-palm, *arbol del viajero, arbre de voyageur*

Strelitziaceae (bird-of-paradise family)

Ravenala on the grounds of the Westin Hotel, St. John, in February. This specimen was about 25 ft. (7.6 m) tall, with a main trunk diameter of 12 in. (30 cm) below the leaf sheath.

This relative of banana is planted as an ornamental in the V.I. and south Florida. Sure to be noticed, it is readily identified by its banana-like, very long leaves spreading like a huge hand fan in a single plane. The evergreen tree is native only to Madagascar and is the only species in the genus *Ravenala*. It is found on all the major Virgin Islands and in south Florida; it has not escaped cultivation.

Form. Travelers-tree grows to 40 ft. (12 m) or more in height and can have trunk diameters of over 12 in. (30 cm). Leaf spread can exceed the height. The trunk does not form branches, but the tree tends to form clumps unless sprouts around the base are removed.

Leaves and bark. Trees usually have 20 or fewer leaves. Petioles are up to 10 ft. (3 m) long and the leaf blades 5–10 ft. (1.5–3 m) long and 2–3 ft. (0.6–1 m) wide. Petioles arise from concave sheaths about 2 ft. (0.6 m) long. Their alternate arrangement gives a woven look to the fan's center. Wind usually tears the leaves between the veins. The lower, oldest leaves turn yellow to brown, droop and break off above the sheath, giving the upper trunk a ratty look. The residual sheaths gradually weather away, leaving a relatively smooth ring around the trunk. Bark is brown or gray, fissuring and becoming rough with age; it is interrupted horizontally by the leaf rings.

Flowers are large bird-of-paradise-like clusters that are borne on single stalks between leaf sheaths. The clusters are 2 ft. (0.6 m) or more long. Each consists of about 8 light green canoe-shaped scales 12–18 in. (30–46 cm) long and arranged in a single plane. Each sheath has several asymmetric white and blue flowers 6–8 in. (15–20 cm) long. Five stamens, 4–5 in. (10–13 cm) long, arise from the flower center. Flowers contain both male and female organs, and appear several times per year.

Fruit. The fruit is a brown, cylindrical, hard capsule 3–4 in. (7.5–10 cm) long and 1 in. (2.5 cm) wide, containing several seeds in a deep blue hairy matrix; each seed is about 0.4 in. (1 cm) long. The capsules split open along three seams when mature.

Flower structure after petals have turned brown (February, St. Croix). The overall length of the structure was about 24 in. (61 cm). Inset shows flower structure of the closely related *Strelitzia nicolae,* which is very similar but smaller than that of *R. madagascariensis* (February, St. Croix).

Nearly mature pods of travelers-tree in May, Naples, Florida; inset shows center pod later, after drying out and opening.

Habitat. Travelers-tree grows in partial shade or full sun in a variety of soils, providing they are well drained. It is moderately drought- and wind-resistant but not salt-tolerant.

Uses. *Ravenala madagascariensis* is a showy ornamental. Its common name comes from the fact that thirsty travelers could find water in leaf folds, flower bracts, and hollow leaf bases. In some tropical areas, travelers-tree is used in a variety of ways besides horticulturally. Thus, its seeds reportedly are eaten, sugar is obtained from the sap, the leaves are used for thatching, and the wood is used in construction. Mention at various websites was made of medicinal uses of this plant, but specifics were not found.

Schefflera actinophylla (Endl.) Harms

schefflera, umbrella-tree, octopus-tree, *árbol pulpo, arbre ombrelle*

Araliaceae (ginseng family)

A typical-shaped tree on the campus of the University of the Virgin Islands, St. Thomas, in February. This specimen was about 20 ft. (6 m) tall and over 12 in. (30 cm) in trunk diameter below the branch point.

It is somewhat disconcerting when one first encounters this familiar "houseplant" standing over 25 ft (8 m) tall. The trees, found growing as ornamentals or naturalized in the V.I. and south Florida, are evergreen, readily identified by their (1) growth habit of several thick trunks arising from a single base; (2) very large, palmately compound, shiny green leaves; (3) showy spike clusters of bright red flowers sticking out of the crown; and (4) clusters of round or top-shaped, small, blackish fruits that follow the flowers on the spikes. Native to northern Australia, *S. actinophylla* is now widespread in the world's tropical regions, including south Florida, southern California, Hawaii, and the West Indies. It is common on St. Croix, and found but not especially common on the other major Virgin Islands.

Form. Schefflera is a fast-growing tree. It can achieve heights of 40 ft. (12 m) and trunk base diameters of over 12 in. (30 cm). The crown is dense and showy.

Leaves are simple and alternate, 2–3 ft. (0.6–0.9 m) long or longer, including the petiole, arranged in spirals on the branches. The leaflets (usually 7–12) are up to 12 in. (30 cm) long.

Flower spikes arise terminally, radiating out to form clusters 2–3 ft. (0.6–0.9 m) in diameter. Flowers are borne in round 0.75-in. (2 cm)-diameter heads along the spike stem, each head on a dark purple stalk.

These leaves were about 24 in. (61 cm) long, including petioles.

Fruits follow the flowers, are about the same size, and are also borne on the spikes in tight clusters.

Habitat. Schefflera prefers full sun and moist, well-drained soils, but is tolerant of shade and various soils. It is only moderately drought-resistant and is not salt-tolerant. Its dense crown also catches wind and the stems can break or split apart at the collar.

Flower spikes in crown in February, St. Croix; inset shows close-up of flower buds and flowers.

Uses. This tree makes an attractive and effective screen. However, it has escaped cultivation, and in south Florida it is now considered a serious invasive. It and closely related species are popular house plants in temperate regions of the world. No reports of uses in folk medicines were found. The leaves contain oxalates that can be fatal when ingested, and allergic reactions to the plant have been reported.

Spikes of fruit clusters at Key West, Florida, in December.

LEAVES SIMPLE, ALTERNATE

Simple leaves arise singly from the twig (or, in some cases, from the trunk or branches). They are said to be alternate when the leaves are not in pairs, but alternate along the twig. Tightly clustered leaves, as in the case of *Crescentia cujete* (calabash-tree) in the image below, are almost always alternate.

Hura crepitans (sandbox)

 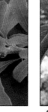

Crescentia cujete (calabash-tree)

Annona squamosa (sweetsop)

Anacardium occidentale L.

cashew, *marañon, pajuil, cajuil, acajou*

Anacardiaceae (cashew family)

Well-formed tree, about 20 ft. (6 m) tall and 12 in. (30 cm) in basal diameter, on the Caneel Bay resort grounds, St. John, in May. Insets show bark from young (left) and old trees.

This tree produces the world's number-one nut crop. Major producing countries are Vietnam and India. It is native to northeast Brazil but has been planted widely in the world's tropics where it has escaped, as in the V.I. Cashew is evergreen, identified by its: (1) prominently veined, leathery, deep green leaves to 6 in. (15 cm) long and 3 in. (8 cm) across; (2) milky sap that is exuded from cut twigs; (3) tiny flowers and unusual fruits, one or the other usually present all year. Cashew is in the same plant family as mango and pistachio—and poison ivy. Indeed, the cashew nut shell is quite toxic. Cashew is found but is not abundant on the major Virgin Islands or south Florida. It is not grown commercially in either location.

Form. Cashews are small trees, generally 10–20 ft. (3–6 m) high, but under the most favorable conditions may reach 40 ft. (12 m). Trunk diameters may exceed 10 in. (25 cm).

Leaves and bark. Leaves are simple, alternate, with smooth margins and short petioles. The light gray to brown bark becomes rough and fissured with age.

Flowers are less than 0.3 in. (8 mm) long and broad, with five pink petals. They are yellow-green at first but turn reddish with time. They occur in terminal clusters 4–19 in. (10–48 cm) long and almost as broad. Both male and bisexual flowers are present in the same clusters. Flowers and fruit may occur on the same tree at the same time.

New leaves are nearly red. The largest leaves here were about 6 in. (15 cm) long; image taken in February.

Fruits are odd-looking, especially as they mature. The actual fruit is a single terminal shell-encased, dark-colored nut, and the yellow or red pear-shaped "cashew-apple" is an enlarged and fleshy stalk of the mature fruit. This fruit-stalk has yellow flesh and is edible. The nut shells have inner and outer layers with a spongy layer between that is infused with a caustic and toxic oil. The nuts must be roasted to remove the oil before they are edible. When mature, the entire apple-nut body falls to the ground, where it can be harvested by hand.

Individual flowers photographed in March were about 0.25 in. (0.6 cm) across.

Habitat. Cashews are hardy trees, able to withstand a variety of soils and moisture regimes, although they prefer hot tropical lowlands that have a distinct dry season and well-drained soil. They are only partially salt-tolerant, but resist drought and do well on sandy sites.

Uses. Cashew nuts are nutritional, being especially rich in vitamin B1 and iron. The fleshy fruit-stalks of cashew, like the roasted nuts, are produced commercially. The former are eaten raw, and also made into jams, jellies, etc. The taste is said to resemble that of pineapple, but is more tangy. The cashew apples are richer in vitamin C than citrus fruits. The tree has other uses as well. The oil, though toxic, is a valuable by-product of the nut industry; "cardol" oil dries to a tough film and can be made into very hard plastics. It is or has been imported into the U.S. and other countries for a variety of industrial uses, including the manufacture

Mature fruit, showing cashew "apple" above the cashew nut-containing black shell; the fruit, including the fleshy part, was about 4 in. (10 cm) long. Tiny flowers are visible if one looks closely; inset shows a close-up of a flower in May.

of brake liners, paints and varnishes. Cashew wood is of medium density and weight, and attractively figured. It has been used some in construction, but the tree is too small for commercial wood production. Cashew "apple" juice, tree sap, and cardol oil have been reported to have many medicinal properties. Folk remedies include treatment of diabetes, thrush, toothache, diarrhea, skin infections, warts, worms, and several other problems. *Note: Seed coat contains toxic and caustic oil.*

Annona muricata L.

soursop, *guanábana, graviola, corossol*

Annonaceae (annona family)

Two-stemmed small tree (20 ft., 6 m tall) by Queen Mary Highway on St. Croix in March.

This widely cultivated and handsome little tree has a popular large edible fruit, and produces a myriad of potentially useful chemicals. It is identified by its: (1) attractive, often fairly large leaves growing in two rows along twigs; (2) spicy fragrance of the leaves when crushed; (3) distinctive flowers, which are almost spherical, with three yellow-green fleshy outer petals; and (4) unusual fruit, which is large, green, fleshy, and covered with soft "spines." Soursop is found throughout the West Indies, including the V.I., where it has escaped. It is found, but not common, in south Florida. Flowers and fruit can usually be found throughout the year in the V.I. and south Florida. The species is thought to have originated in the West Indies and northern South America. However, it is not considered native to the V.I. or south Florida. A closely related species, *A. glabra* (pond-apple) is common in Florida and found in the V.I., where it is uncommon.

Form. Soursop has a single trunk, branching near the ground, or multiple trunks. With a bushy crown, the tree has a pleasing overall form. It may reach 23 ft. (7 m) in height and trunk diameter of 6 in. (15 cm).

Leaves and bark. Leaves are dark green, shiny, simple, and alternate. They have short petioles and are broadest beyond the middle. They are often large, to 10 in. (25 cm) long and 3 in. (8 cm) across. The brown bark, relatively smooth on young trunks, becomes scaly with age.

Leaves, about 6 in. (15 cm) long, were photographed in February on St. John.

Flowers are produced singly anywhere on the trunk, branches and twigs, each on a short, stout green stalk. They are about 1.5 in. (4 cm) in length, and across the fully open petals, and exude a strong unpleasant, pungent odor.

Flowers, photographed in November, were about 1.5 in. (4 cm) in diameter.

Fruits follow the flowers on various parts of the tree. They weigh 2–5 pounds (1–2.3 kg), and are 6–8 in. (15–20 cm) long and about 4 in. (10 cm) in diameter, usually shaped like a large bent avocado. The skin is bitter and inedible. Oblong shiny black seeds 0.5–.6 in. (1.3–1.6 cm) long are embedded in the white stringy flesh. Most people, including the author, think the fruit and its juice are very tasty—sweet, not sour as the English name implies. The seeds are toxic.

Habitat. Soursop is drought-resistant, prefers alkaline (limestone) soils, full sun or bright shade, and is mildly salt-tolerant.

Uses. The fruit and juice and products made from them (ice cream, sherbet, syrup) are increasingly available, especially in tropical markets, and are becoming popular in temperate regions. Natives of the V.I. use the fruit in small amounts to quiet crying babies at night. Leaves, flowers, fruit, seeds, bark, and roots have all been used in folk medicines for a wide variety of ailments, including treatments for worms and other parasites, fever, diarrhea and even diabetes and hepatitis. As mentioned, the tree provides a rich assortment of chemicals that at the time of publication are being studied for pharmacological, insecticidal, and other uses; a number of patents have been issued. The wood is soft, lightweight, not durable, and little used.

This fruit, photographed in November, was 6 in. (15 cm) long.

Note: Seeds contain a potent toxin.

Annona squamosa L.

sugar-apple, sweetsop, cachiman, *anón, pomme cannelle*

Annonaceae

Sugar-apple tree, about 20 ft. (6 m) tall and 6 in. (15 cm) in trunk diameter at the base, on the campus of the University of the Virgin Islands, St. Thomas, in February.

Sugar-apple is widely cultivated in orchards in tropical areas around the world for its tasty and nutritious fruit. It is a small, deciduous tree identified by its: (1) zigzag twigs, red when young, becoming brown; (2) leaves, which occur in two rows on opposite sides of the twigs, fragrant when crushed; (3) its flowers and fruit, both of which are present essentially all year in the V. I. and much of the year in south Florida. Widely grown, usually as single trees in the V.I., it is unfortunately plagued there by an insect-borne fungal disease that causes many of the fruits to mummify. Everywhere sugar-apple is grown, including the V.I., it has escaped and become naturalized. It is fairly common on St. Croix, St. Thomas, and Tortola, and is found but not common on St. John, Virgin Gorda, or in the Florida Keys. The geographical origin of *A. squamosa* is uncertain.

Form. *A. squamosa* is a small tree that grows only to 10–20 ft. (3–6 m) tall with trunk diameters to about 6 in. (15 cm). It sometimes has a single main trunk, but often branches near the ground. The open crown is somewhat disheveled-looking. The brown bark is relatively smooth, becoming slightly fissured with age.

The longest leaves were about 5 in. (13 cm).

Leaves are simple, alternate, smooth-margined, and 2–5.5 in. (6–13 cm) long. They have short petioles. The tree loses it leaves briefly in late winter.

Flowers are 0.6–1 in. (1.5–2.5 cm) long, and have three thick petals and a purplish dot at the inside base. They are borne singly or in lateral clusters. Blooming occurs throughout the year.

Fruits are apple-shaped aggregates with knobby surfaces, resembling artichokes. They are yellow-green or purple, 2.5–4 in. (6–10 cm) in diameter. The yellow-green varieties blacken when rubbed or bruised. When ripe they are easily broken open

Newly formed fruit inside a spent flower.

Flower and flower buds on a twig in February. Flowers were about 1 in (2.5 cm) across.

to reveal the cream-colored, edible—and highly prized—pulp. The blackish seeds (20–40/fruit), about 0.5 in. (1.3 cm) long, are embedded in the pulp, but are easy to remove.

Habitat. Sugar-apple does best in dry areas, having a high drought tolerance. It prefers full sun, but can tolerate some shade. Salt tolerance is said to be moderate. It grows in a variety of well-drained soils.

Mature fruit in tree in February.

Uses. Sugar-apple is one of the most popular fruits in India and in Brazil, where it is abundant. It is grown commercially in India and many other locales, and is readily available in tropical markets worldwide. Seedless varieties have been developed, as well as the varieties that bear purple fruit. The wood is light, soft and weak, and not used. Various parts of the tree have been used in folk medicines, for example to treat diarrhea, cramps, spasm, fever, skin lesions, and colds. Powder made from the seeds is used to kill and repel insects. Modern chemical studies have identified many bioactive compounds in *A. squamosa* extracts.

Purple variety in November.

Note: Seeds are acrid and poisonous.

Bauhinia variegata L.

poor man's orchid, orchid tree, bauhinia, mountain ebony, *palo de orquideas, arbre à orchidées*

Bauhinia monandra Kurz

poor man's orchid, butterfly bauhinia, *mariposa, arbre aux orchidées*

Fabaceae (pea family)

B. variegata

B. monandra

This large specimen of *B. variegata*, in a park in Saint Petersburg, Florida, in December, was about 40 ft. (12 m) tall and 15 in. (38 cm) or more in diameter below the fork.

Poor man's orchids (both *Bauhinia* species above), are commonly planted in the V.I. for their beautiful pink/purple flowers and attractive foliage. In south Florida, *B. variegata* and the closely related third species, *B. purpurea,* are commonly planted ornamentals. All three species are identified by their: (1) oddly two-lobed, dark, dull green leaves (not seen in other trees in this book); (2) beautiful orchidlike flowers, usually present much of the year; (3) long, persisting pods; and (4) disheveled branching pattern, giving them a somewhat disorganized look, especially when young. These species are native to northern India, Vietnam, and southern China, and have been planted widely in other tropical areas. In the V.I. and south Florida, they have escaped in some areas. The genus *Bauhinia* contains several other species used in south Florida and elsewhere as ornamentals.

Form. These *Bauhinias* are small trees to 40 ft. (12 m) tall, with spreading crowns 10–20 ft. (3–6 m) across or wider. They usually have single trunks up to 12 in. (30 cm) in diameter.

Leaves. The attractive leaves are simple and alternate, with petioles 1–2 in. (2.5–5 cm) long, and blades mostly 2–5 in. (5–13 cm) long and broad. Leaves are fairly leathery.

Leaves and pods in crown of *B. monandra* (left), on St. Croix in November; stem and leaves of *B. variegata* (right), on St. Croix in February.

Flowers, clustered at the ends of twigs, are fragrant, showy, and reminiscent of orchids. Five wavy-edged petals, each about 2 in. (5 cm) long and up to 1 in. (2.5 cm) wide, are attached to a narrow green basal tube, and 1–7 long, whitish, upward-curving stamens protrude from the flowers. Flowering is nearly constant, but the trees are especially showy in early spring. A white-flowered variety of *B. variegata* is found in south Florida. In *B. monandra*, the center petal is streaked with purple spots.

Flowers and immature fruit pods of *B. variegata* in crown; insets show close-ups of flowers, about 3 in. in diameter (*B. monandra* on left); photographs made in February in the V.I.

Fruits are 5–12 in. (13–30 cm) long, flat (*B. variegata*) to somewhat cylindrical (*B. monandra*), about 0.75 in. (1.9 cm) wide, and green, becoming dark brown. They occur in clusters, and split open when mature to release several seeds. The pods and hulls may persist for months, and are considered unattractive. Some sterile hybrids produce the showy flowers but no pods.

Fruit and seeds of *B. monandra* (top, in November) and fruit of *B. variegata*, in February.

Habitat. *Bauhinia variegata*, and probably the other *Bauhinia* species as well, like acidic soils, and are not especially salt-tolerant. They can tolerate light shade, and are drought-resistant.

Uses. The *Bauhinias* are used mainly as ornamentals, but the young leaves, flowers, and fruit of several species have been used as food and fodder. In south Florida, these species are considered undesirable invasives in some areas. Many folk medicinal uses of leaves, bark, flowers and fruit have been described for the three species here, including treatments for cough, sore throats, skin diseases, hemorrhoids, and even malaria, worms, cancer, and diabetes. The trees make a variety of complex chemicals, some of which have been shown in modern studies to have medical potential. The bark, which is easily removed, has been used as cordage. The wood of some species of *Bauhinia* is useful, but the trees are usually too small to be important for timber purposes.

Bourreria succulenta Jacq.

pigeon-berry, bodywood, chink, strongbark, *palo de vaca, acomat côte-lette*

Boraginaceae (borage family)

One of the most common trees in dry areas of the V.I., pigeon-berry is native to the V.I. and south Florida. It is identified by its (1) attractive leaves, quite variable in size; (2) sizeable clusters of small, fragrant white flowers; and (3) small red-orange fruits. Both flowers and fruits are usually present year-round, making this tree easy to identify. It is evergreen except in periods of extended drought. The tree is found throughout the West Indies (except the Bahamas), in south Florida (where some consider it endangered), and northern South America.

Relatively tall tree at Magen's Beach, St. Thomas, in February; this tree was 44 ft. (13 m) tall x 7 in. (18 cm) dbh.

Form. *Bourreria succulenta* is a small tree, growing to 40 ft. (12 m) tall, usually with a single trunk, and 8 in. (20 cm) or sometimes more in diameter. The branches can be spreading or drooping, forming in both cases a fairly compact, rounded crown. The trunk is often sinewy or slightly fluted.

Leaves and bark. The simple, alternate leaves are 1.5–5 in. (4–13 cm) long and 1–3 in. (2.5–5 cm) broad, on petioles about 0.5 in. (1.3 cm) long. The brown-gray bark becomes fissured on older trunks.

Leaves of pigeon-berry vary considerably in size.

Flowers occur in flat-topped, erect, much-branched white clusters, terminally or laterally on twigs. The clusters are 2–8 in. (5–20 cm) across and in height. They turn brown before falling.

Fruits, about 0.5 in. (1.3 cm) in diameter, are green when immature but red-orange to red and edible when ripe. Each contains four brown, ridged seeds. Fruits are eaten by birds, which spread the seeds.

Habitat. Pigeon-berry is drought-tolerant, salt-tolerant, and fairly resistant to wind, so it has advantages in dry coastal sites. It prefers full sun and slightly alkaline soils.

Flower and bud cluster and flower detail, photographed in February.

Uses. This native species is used in horticultural plantings because of its flowers and fruit, and its attractiveness to birds and bees. Concoctions of the bark, fruit, and leaves have been used as folk remedies for thrush and other oral inflammations, and the fruit supposedly has aphrodisiac properties. The wood is hard and reportedly attractive, but the tree is too small for its wood to be used for much besides firewood.

Photographed in February.

Bucida buceras L.

black-olive, oxhorn bucida, gregorywood, *ucar, gregre, bois gli-gli*

Combretaceae (combretum family)

Venerable old tree in Cramer Park, east end, St. Croix, approximately 40 ft. (12 m) tall and over 4 ft. (1.2 m) in trunk diameter at the narrowest level. Photographed in January.

This large tree, which is not a true olive, is identified by its (1) wide-spreading crown of horizontal, often drooping branches and many-forked twigs; (2) small leaves that are borne in whorls on twig spurs; (3) dense, usually evergreen, crown; and (4) spikes of tiny flowers and fruits, both of which are usually present. Black-olive is native to tropical America, including the V.I., and perhaps to the Florida Keys. The tree is found from south Florida through the West Indies down to Guadeloupe, and from southern Mexico down into northern South America. It is common on all the major Virgin Islands, perhaps less so on St. Thomas. It is a widely used landscape tree in south Florida.

Form. Black-olive can grow to over 100 ft. (30 m) tall and the dense crown can be even wider. Its single trunk can reach 5 ft. (1.5 m) or more in diameter. It is among the largest trees encountered in the V.I. In south Florida it is a smaller tree.

Leaves are simple and alternate and vary greatly in size, from 1–4 in. (2.5–10 cm) long and 0.5–2 in. (1.3–5 cm) across. They are dark green on the upper surface and yellowish green below. The twigs of some trees have small paired spines.

Flowers occur in spikelike clusters that are borne along stalks arising among the leaves. The profusion of flowers in the spring creates quite a display.

Nearly mature fruit clusters nestled in leaves, showing insect galls ("ox-horns"), photographed in March.

Fruits are shaped like tiny, five-sided urns, dull green turning somewhat brownish. Each contains a single seed. If attacked by a certain common eryphide mite (*Eriophyes buceras*), the fruits develop a long, slender, bean-shaped gall ("oxhorn"); these are common enough to have spawned one of the tree's common names.

Habitat. Black-olive does best in rich, moist, well-drained soils, but is tolerant of most soil types. The species is wind- and drought-resistant, and is salt-tolerant. It grows well on dry coastal sites.

Flower cluster photographed in March.

Uses. *B. buceras* wood is attractive, and one of the heaviest known. It is stable and resists decay and insects, making it useful for outdoor applications. It can be finished to a high polish, but its hardness keeps it from being widely used by woodcrafters. The tree is used horticulturally because of its beauty, the shade it creates, and its tolerance of pollution. It is a common street tree in south Florida. The abundant flowers attract bees. Black-olive bark has been used in the tanning of hides. Resin has been used to treat swollen glands and as an antidote to manchineel poisoning (see *Hipponane mancinella*). Chemicals produced by the tree are being studied for anti-tumor properties.

Callistemon citrinus (Curtis) Skeels

bottlebrush, red bottlebrush, crimson bottlebrush, lemon bottlebrush, *limpiatubos, rince-bouteille, goupillon*

Myrtaceae (myrtle family)

Nicely formed tree in west-central St. Croix near Centerline Road in May, about 20 ft. (6 m) tall and 11 in. (28 cm) in trunk diameter.

Bottlebrush, a native of Australia, is widely planted in the V.I. and south Florida as an evergreen ornamental. It is easily recognized by its (1) bright red cylindrical flower clusters shaped like bottlebrushes; (2) the small, hard, round, woody seed capsules huddled around the twigs behind the flowering areas; and (3) the faint lemon fragrance of crushed leaves. Both flowers and fruits are present essentially all year, although the number of flowers on a given tree at any time varies greatly. Another species of *Callistemon*, *C. viminalis*, is called weeping bottlebrush. Both of these species are landscape plants.

Form. *Callistemon citrinus* gets to be a small tree to 30 ft. (9 m) tall and 18 in. (46 cm) or more in diameter but often is encountered as a large shrub. It has a nicely rounded form, often with multiple trunks, and branches bearing leaf-rich twigs with flowers and fruit.

Leaves are simple and alternate, but spread in all directions from the twigs; they are 1.25–2.5 in. (3–6 cm) long and about 0.25 in. (0.6 cm) wide.

Flowers, in cylindrical clusters 2–4 in. (5–10 cm) long and 1.5 in. (4 cm) in diameter, derive their color from the long stamens.

Fruit capsules are nearly spherical cups about 0.25 in. (0.6 cm) in diameter, and contain many tiny seeds. The closed fruits stay on the twigs for at least several months before opening.

Habitat. Bottlebrush is tolerant of drought, salt, and poor soil, so it grows in many habitats. It prefers full sun. This species grows in most parts of Florida.

Uses. *Callistemon citrinus* is mainly used as an ornamental in most tropical areas. However, chemicals made by the tree are being investigated for herbicidal properties and for potential in human medicine. The light brown, heavy, hard wood has been used in Australia for tool handles and related items.

1 in.
2.5 cm

Leaves, flower, and fruits on a twig (February).

A close-up of the stamen-dominated flowers.

Abundant flower clusters of *C. viminalis* near Homestead, Florida, in April.

Canella winterana (L.) Gaertn.

caneel, canella, wild cinnamon, *barbasco, canellier blanc*

Canellaceae (canella family)

Small tree at Magens Bay on St. Thomas in February, approximately 17 ft. (5 m) tall and 6 in. (15 cm) in trunk diameter near the base.

Native to the V.I. and south Florida, caneel is not an abundant tree, but its clusters of red flowers and berries invite a closer look. The small evergreen tree is identified by its (1) attractive, somewhat leathery leaves clustered at branch ends; (2) flowers and berries, present irregularly through the year; and (3) spicy cinnamon fragrance of the crushed leaves. Because it is used as an ornamental, specimens can be found without too much difficulty. *Canella winterana* is found throughout the West Indies, the Bahamas, and south Florida.

Form. *Canella winterana* can attain a height of nearly 50 ft. (15 m) and trunk diameter of 8 in. (20 cm), but is usually quite a bit smaller. It has an attractive, rounded or pyramidal, dense crown on a single trunk when it has space. It sometimes forms thickets, however, where it has a more crowded appearance.

Leaves and bark. Leaves are alternate, 1–5 in. (2.5–13 cm) long and 0.5–1.5 in. (1.3–3.8 cm) across, leathery, and shiny green. The bark is dark gray or brown, becoming fissured and rough with age.

Fruit and leaves in February; largest leaves were 5 in. (13 cm) long, and the fruit about 0.4 in. (1 cm) in diameter.

Flowers are borne in terminal clusters surrounded by leaves and unopened green and purple buds. The buds open to reveal bright dark red flowers with five petals surrounding yellow-orange centers. Flowers are only about 0.25 in. (0.6 cm) across and long, but the clusters are 1 in. (2.5 cm) or more across, and showy.

Fruits are round berries, about 0.4 in. (1 cm) in diameter, green becoming bright red, fleshy, with two to several small black seeds.

Habitat. Caneel is drought-resistant as well as fairly salt- and wind-resistant, and is found in drier coastal limestone habitats.

Uses. The yellow inner bark has the flavor of cinnamon and cloves. It was once dried and sold as a spice and for medicinal uses under the name "Canella bark." Various parts of the tree have been used in folk remedies to treat many maladies, including rheumatism, sore throat, and fever; it has also been used as an abortifacient. The green berries, gathered and dried, are said to taste like black pepper. Leaves and stems proved to be toxic to poultry in feeding trials on St. Croix.

Flowers, photographed in Key West, Florida, in April, were about 0.25 in. (0.6 cm) across.

Indeed, crushed leaves and twigs have been used to stupefy fish for easy harvesting—as is the case with fishpoison tree (*Piscidia carthagenensis*). The wood is hard and heavy, with olive-brown-colored sapwood and nearly black heartwood. It has been used for fence posts, but the tree is usually too small to be used for wood products.

Capparis cynophallophora L.

black caper, Jamaica caper, *burro prieto, bois noir*

Capparidaceae (caper family)

Open-grown tree in May at St. George Village Botanical Garden, St. Croix, approximately 18 ft. (5.5 m) tall and 6 in. (15 cm) in trunk diameter above the swollen base.

Food capers are pickled flower buds of Mediterranean relatives of black caper. *Capparis cynophallophora* flower buds have a similar flavor, but are bitter. Black caper is native to south Florida, and one of six caper species native to the V.I. A closely related species, also native to the V.I., is white caper, *C. indica*, nearly indistinguishable from black caper. Black caper is identified from its (1) leaves, which are folded and bronze when young; (2) form, usually involving multiple trunks and a dense crown; (3) clusters of showy, strange-smelling flowers, white, becoming purple and consisting mostly of stamens; and (4) cylindrical seed pods to 8 in. (20 cm) long, which split open to reveal scarlet pulp with embedded seeds. Flowers and fruits are present on at least some trees all year. Black caper is found through the West Indies, southern Mexico, and Central America south to Panama. It is common on all the V.I., though perhaps less so on St. Croix. A vinelike caper, *C. flexuosa*, with showy white flowers, is more common on all the islands.

Form. Black caper is an attractive evergreen tree that can attain a height of about 20 ft. (6 m) and a trunk diameter of about 6 in. (15 cm).

Leaves and bark. The simple, alternate leaves are shiny green above and silvery brown below. They are smooth-margined, 2–4 in. (5–10 cm) long and 0.5–1.5 in. (1.3–4 cm) across; petioles are short. Juvenile leaves on very young trees may be much longer and narrower, and almost black. The bark is dark gray to dark brown, smooth at first, but becoming fissured with age.

Leaves and buds at a twig end; leaves were 2–3 in. (5–7.5 cm) long; photographed in April.

Flower clusters occur near the ends of twigs. The showy individual flowers contain both male and female parts. Each has four pink-white petals about 0.5 in. (1.3 cm) long and numerous protruding stamens. They are pollinated by moths. Appearing just after nightfall, the flowers wilt early the next day.

Fruits are 3–8 in. (7.5–20 cm) long and about 0.3 in. (0.8 cm) in diameter, borne on long stalks. Green, becoming brown at maturity, they split open on one side at maturity; seeds are about 0.25 in. (0.6 cm) long. Birds eat the pulp and probably spread the seeds.

Flower in tree with stamens 2 in. (5 cm) long; inset shows *Capparis flexuosa* flower in May, about 2 in. (5 cm) across.

Habitat. Black caper is a part of dry coastal thickets. It is a hardy tree, being tolerant of salt, drought, and wind. It grows in various types of soils.

Uses. *Capparis cynophyllophora* is an attractive tree used in landscape plantings. Its dense crown and resistance to very high winds have led to its use in windbreaks. The tree is too small to be used for its wood, except for fence posts and firewood. Root decoctions have been used to treat herpes, skin diseases, edema, and intestinal worms.

Mature fruit pods in tree, the open ones revealing the bright red interiors; pods, photographed in May, averaged about 7 in. (18 cm) in length.

Cecropia schreberiana Miq.

trumpet-tree, cecropia, *yagrumbo hembra, bois canon*

Cecropiaceae (cecropia family)

Open-grown tree at The Fruit and Spice Park, Homestead, Florida, in April. It was approximately 34 ft. (10 m) tall and 12 in. (30 cm) in trunk diameter below the branch point. Inset shows typical young trees on a disturbed roadside on Bordeaux Mt., St. John, in March. These trees were 20–30 ft (6–9 m) tall and 5–6 in. (13–15 cm) in dbh.

Trumpet-tree is often the first to colonize areas where forests have been destroyed by hurricanes or other disturbances. Its seeds are produced in very large numbers and spread by birds and bats. They lie dormant in forest soils, germinating when the canopy is opened, giving rise to a rapidly growing, unusual-looking tree. Trumpet-tree is recognized by its (1) thin spreading crown of upward-turning stout branches; (2) exceptionally large, lobed leaves clustered on long petioles at branch ends, dark green above and whitish below; (3) characteristic, elongated fruits which are found year-round; and (4) hollow young branches. It is native to the V.I. and other West Indies islands and to tropical areas of the Americas. In some areas it is considered an invasive tree. It is fairly common on St. Croix, St. John, and Tortola, perhaps less so on St. Thomas. Apparently, it is not found on Virgin Gorda or in south Florida. However, *C. peltata* and *C. palmata* occur in south Florida and are so similar to *C. schreberiana* that all three species can be recognized with the information above.

Form. Trees may reach a height of 70 ft. (21 m) and trunk diameter of 24 in. (61 cm), but small young trees are seen more often.

Leaves. Leaves are 12–30 in. (30–76 cm) across, on stout hollow petioles 12–24 in. (30–61 cm) long. The 7–11 rounded lobes have wavy margins. Leaf buds, at the ends of branches, are long, pointed, and red. The dry, fallen leaves, always present under the trees, crackle when walked on.

Flowers. Male and female flowers occur on different trees. Both are very small and occur in dense, pale yellow, narrow cylindrical clusters. Male cylinders occur in groups of 15 or more at the end of a 2–3 in. (5–7.6 cm) stalk; each cylinder has a stalk about 0.5 in. (1.3 cm) long. Female flower clusters are similar but occur in groups of 2–5. Trees bloom all year in the V.I.

Fruits. When ripe, the edible grayish fruits are 2.5–4 in. (6.3–10 cm) long and about 0.5 in. (1.3 cm) in diameter. Their surface is dotted with numerous tiny seeds, each about 0.06 in. (1.5 mm) long. Seeds number over 1 million per pound (2.2 million per kilogram). Fruits are jellylike and sweet.

Habitat. *C. schreberiana* prefers full sun, and is not tolerant of drought or salt. Usually found in moist areas of the islands, it provides a relatively open, protective canopy for longer-lived trees to develop. Its presence is an indicator of past forest disturbance.

Uses. The wood of trumpet-tree is lightweight, and neither durable nor strong. Even so, it is used for plywood core stock, particleboard, match sticks, boxes, light construction, etc. The hollow young branches have been used to make musical instruments ("trumpets"). In the V.I. and Puerto Rico, the hollow branches harbor stinging ants. Leaves, roots, bark, and the tree's thin, caustic latex have been used in folk medicines to treat fever, asthma, Parkinson's Disease, and epilepsy, and to help heal wounds, remove warts, provide a poultice to reduce swelling, and to prepare a diuretic.

This leaf was 16 in. (41 cm) across.

Branch end in crown showing new and mature leaves, male flower cylinders, and buds, in February, St. Croix. The male flower cluster was approximately 3 in. (7.5 cm) across.

Nearly mature fruit clusters high in a crown in May on St. Croix.

Citrus spp.

orange tree, lemon, lime, grapefruit, key lime, *toronja, China, pamplemousse, orange douce,* and many other names

Rutaceae (rue family)

Well-formed orange tree on the grounds of the Lawaetz Museum, St. Croix, in May. This tree was about 19 ft. (6 m) tall and 6 in. (15 cm) in trunk diameter just below the branch point. Inset shows lichen-encrusted bark.

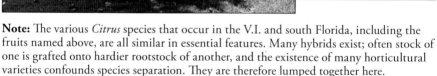

Note: The various *Citrus* species that occur in the V.I. and south Florida, including the fruits named above, are all similar in essential features. Many hybrids exist; often stock of one is grafted onto hardier rootstock of another, and the existence of many horticultural varieties confounds species separation. They are therefore lumped together here.

Easily recognized by the familiar fruits hanging on the evergreen trees, *Citrus* spp. also can be recognized by other features, including their (1) shiny, attractive leaves with rounded, shallow teeth on their margins, and usually, winged petioles; (2) petioles jointed at the leaf bases; (3) (usually) sharp spines at the nodes between the green twigs and the branches; and (4) flowers and fruit present much of the year. The various *Citrus* species are native to Asia but cultivated so long and so extensively that their exact origin is obscure.

Form. Citrus trees have one to a few trunks joined at the ground line. They attain heights of 10–30 ft. (3–9 m) and trunk diameters to 6 in. (15 cm) or more. Their crowns are often compact, spreading, and quite attractive.

Leaves and bark. The simple, alternate leaves are 2–6 in. (5–15 cm) long, oblong, and have rounded ends. Petioles are about 0.5 in. (1.3 cm) long. Bark is usually gray-brown and finely fissured.

Leaves and immature orange on a twig; the orange was about 3 in. (7.5 cm) in diameter. Image taken in February on St. Croix.

Flowers are up to 2 in. (5 cm) in diameter. Those of various citrus species have similar basic structures. Each has 4–5 waxy white elliptical petals surrounding a white cup with protruding stamens, yellow en masse. Flowers have a pleasantly strong, sweet aroma.

Thorns, leaves, and very young fruit. Image taken in February on St. Croix.

Fruits. The familiar edible fruits vary in size, taste, and color. In the tropics they usually do not change from green to the familiar orange-to-yellow color, which requires cool nights. But they taste the same. Mature fruits are found year-round, and may remain on the trees for several weeks. They contain seeds varying in number from many to none, the size and shapes of which are familiar to all.

Habitat. Citrus trees prefer full sun and moist, well-drained soils, and are not salt- or drought-tolerant. They actually thrive better in subtropical climates as in Florida than in the V.I., but are quite frost-sensitive.

Flowers photographed on St. John in February.

Uses. In the V.I., the *Citrus* species are planted mostly as fruit-bearing ornamentals. In other parts of the tropical world, the valuable crop trees are grown commercially in pampered plantations. The oil of some fruit rinds is used as flavoring and in various industrial applications, including soaps and cleansers. Citrus flavors are used in many food and medicinal products. The essential oil of orange is used in Western Africa to treat dysentery, fever, headache, and oral infections. Extracts of various plant parts have been widely used in folk medicines to treat everything from headache to liver ailments. Citrus trees are good honey plants.

Coccoloba uvifera (L.) L.

sea-grape, grape, *uva de playa, raisinier bord-de-mer*

Polygonaceae (buckwheat family)

Sea-grape trees on the northeast shore of St. Croix, photographed in January; the tallest tree here was over 20 ft. (6 m), with a trunk diameter of 7 in. (18 cm).

Sea-grape is almost everyone's favorite beach tree and one of the best known. It is easily recognized by its (1) usual location on sandy beaches; (2) growth habit; (3) big, round, leathery leaves, usually with reddish veins; (4) spikes of pale yellow flowers; (5) bunches of green (becoming purple) clusters of "grapes;" and (6) smooth, mottled bark. Flowers and fruits are found through the year. The dense crown of sea-grape provides welcome beach shade to sunburned tourists. *Coccoloba uvifera* is native to the V.I. and south Florida, and probably throughout the American tropics. It has been widely planted elsewhere. It is common on all the V.I. and in south Florida.

Form. The form that sea-grape trees take varies with the habitat. On dry wind-swept beaches it may be short and hug the ground. On more protected sites it can become a tree up to 50 ft. (15 m) tall and over 24 in. (61 cm) in trunk diameter. Its form is usually between these extremes. The tree often has multiple leaning and contorted trunks, or a single trunk that branches near the ground. Even when it has a single dominant trunk, it usually leans. The crown is dense and usually spreads to a greater width than the tree's height.

Leaves here were 4–6 in. (10–15 cm) in diameter.

Leaves and bark. Leaves are simple and alternate, up to 8 in. (20 cm) in diameter, thick and with prominent veins. Leaves have stubby petioles 0.25–0.5 in. (0.6–1.3 cm) long. The bright green leaves may turn red with age. The bark is tan, flaking off in plates to reveal a gray underlayer.

Flower spike in February, approximately 8 in. (20 cm) long. Photo taken on St. Thomas.

Flowers occur in terminal and lateral, upright, slender clusters 4–9 in. (10–23 cm) long. Male and female flower clusters appear similar but occur on separate trees. Individual flowers extend perpendicularly from a central stem.

Fruits are crowded in elongated clusters 4–9 in. (10–23 cm) long; each "grape" is up to 0.75 in. (2 cm) in diameter. Mature ones are edible—sweet and flavorful. Each contains a single elliptical seed about 0.4 in. (1 cm) long. Birds eat the mature fruits and disperse the seeds.

Immature but fully grown fruit cluster with seed, in January on St. Croix.

Habitat. Sea-grape needs full sun, and is resistant to drought, salt, and wind. It thrives on sandy and rocky sea shores, where it is often the dominant plant. It grows most rapidly and reaches its largest size on sites that are protected and receive full sun, combined with well-drained soil and adequate rainfall. Such sites are not common in the V.I., but are perhaps more common in south Florida.

Uses. This species is valued as an ornamental, used singly and in hedges, and as a protector of seashores; in fact, it is illegal to destroy the trees in Florida because of their ecological importance. Sea-grape is so susceptible to drywood termites, however, that planting it close to structures is discouraged. The wood, hard and heavy, is made into bowls and other turned items. The resinous sap, known commercially as West Indian or Jamaican "kino," was once used for tanning hides and dyeing. Extracts of the roots and bark have served as folk remedies for diarrhea, dysentery, and skin itch, and as an astringent.

Conocarpus erectus L.

button-mangrove, buttonwood, *mangle botón, mangle gris*

Combretaceae (combretum family)

Typical multiple-stemmed, leaning button-mangrove, laden with flowers and cones, at the Key West golf course, Florida, in April. The tree was about 21 ft. (6.4 m) tall, with individual trunks 6–12 in. (15–30 cm) in diameter near their bases.

One of the four mangrove trees in the V.I. and south Florida, button-mangrove is always in bloom and always has "cones," making identification relatively straightforward. Characteristics to use include its (1) form—generally leaning, branching near the ground, with a spreading crown; (2) numerous small round clusters of pale yellow-green flowers; (3) rough and stringy bark; (4) simple, alternate leaves; and (5) small reddish cones in clusters. Hardy to the elements, and tolerant of human activities, it is often seen planted in parking lots and along streets. Button-mangrove is native to south Florida, and apparently to most of the West Indies as well. It is found on most of the Caribbean islands and on the east and west shores of tropical Central and South America. The tree is common on all the V.I. and in south Florida.

Form. *Conocarpus erectus* is seldom erect. Many of the trees have multiple trunks and are more shrublike than trees. Single-trunk specimens, however, can get to be 30–40 ft. (9–12 m) tall and 8 in. (20 cm) or greater in trunk diameter. Open-grown trees have a crown of medium density.

Leaves and bark. Leaves are 1–3 in. (2.5–7.5 cm) long, elliptical, pointed on both ends, on short, slightly winged petioles. This is the only mangrove with alternate leaves. Leaves are rather leathery, and their margins are smooth. Bark is gray or brown, becoming rough, furrowed, and somewhat stringy.

Fruit and flower clusters on a twig.

Flowers are tiny, about 0.06 in. (1.6 mm) across, but occur in fragrant, ball-shaped clusters about 0.25 in. (0.6 cm) in diameter borne terminally or laterally. They have short stalks attaching them at points around a central stem that is 1–3 in. (2.5–7.5 cm) long. Most flowers are bisexual, but some trees have only male flowers, and hence no cones.

Fruit. Mature fruits are up to 0.75 in. (2 cm) in length, on short stalks. They are borne in clusters, and each is composed of many scale-like seeds about 0.12 in. (3.2 mm) long.

Leaf attachment detail.

Habitat. Like all mangroves, this one is very tolerant of salt and wet soils. It is usually found on the landward edges of other mangroves, which often grow in the water. Button-mangrove is drought-resistant and it grows in a variety of soil types. It prefers full sun.

Close-up of flower cluster.

Uses. The major value of this species is its role in protecting vulnerable shores from erosion and other damage. It roots from its limbs as they contact the ground, and a new plant follows, often leading to thickets. As mentioned, it is used as a horticultural planting; a silver-blue variety has been developed for this purpose and is common in south Florida. Button-mangrove is not a messy tree, and its often leaning and contorted form is attractive, as are the foliage and fruit. Its wood is hard, heavy, strong, and would be durable except for being susceptible to drywood termites. Even so, the wood has been used for cross ties, fence posts, wood turnings, and boatbuilding, as well as for firewood and charcoal. Bark tannins have been used to tan hides, and extracts of the roots and bark in folk medicines for treating fish poisoning, diabetes, intestinal irritation, colic, bleeding gums, and diarrhea.

Close-up of mature fruit photographed in south Florida in December.

Cordia rickseckeri Mill sp.

orange manjack, black manjack, *San Bartolomé*

Boraginaceae (borage family)

Nearly leafless tree in early March on the Caneel Bay resort grounds, St. John. This tree was about 30 ft. (9 m) tall and 10 in. (25 cm) in diameter below the branches.

2 in.
5 cm

Except during its brief time without leaves, orange manjack is a showy tree, with its orange-veined leaves and clusters of flowers. Flowers and fruit are present just about all year, but flowers are especially abundant in late winter and early spring, and fruit in summer and fall. The tree is identified by its (1) bright orange flowers in broad clusters; (2) green to brown, egg-shaped fruits, also in clusters; and (3) orange-veined leaves, which are very rough on the upper surfaces, smooth-margined, and often have sunken lateral veins. The tree loses its leaves in late winter. An introduced, closely related species, *C. sebestina*, has larger flowers, narrower leaves, and white fruit. Orange manjack is common on all the major Virgin Islands, though perhaps less so on St. Thomas. It apparently is not found in south Florida. *Cordia sebestina* might be native to south Florida, where it is said to be endangered.

Form. *C. rickseckeri* in the open usually has a single trunk—often fluted—and nicely rounded or columnar, attractive crown of medium density. Trees may attain heights of 35 ft. (11 m) and trunk diameters of 14 in. (36 cm).

Leaves and bark. Leaves are alternate and simple, dark green above and lighter below, 3–9 in. (7.5–23 cm) long and 2–4 in. (5–10 cm) wide, with short petioles. The bark is gray, fissured, often with deep long furrows.

Flowers are terminal, in branched clusters. They are trumpet-shaped, about 1.25 in. (3 cm) long and 1 in. (2.5 cm) across, and have short stalks. The color is in the funnel-shaped petal, which has prominent ridges and 5 or 6 rounded lobes at the margin.

Fruits. The fruits are on thin stems. Inside is a thin pulp and a single thick-walled stone seed. Like that of white manjack, this tree's fruit is edible, though hardly palatable.

Habitat. Orange manjack likes full sun and is found in dry coastal forests. It is very salt- and drought-tolerant, and fairly wind-resistant.

Uses. Attractive to hummingbirds as well as humans, this species is often planted as an ornamental. The wood is hard and probably has been used in cabinetry. Its durability is not known. No references to folk remedies based on orange manjack were found.

Leaves on twig, photographed in March, St. Croix.

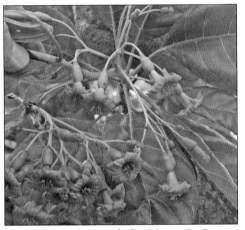

Flower cluster, photographed in May on St. Croix; flowers were about 1.5 in. (3.7 cm) across.

Fruit cluster, photographed in May on St. Croix; each fruit was about 1.5 in. (4 cm) long.

Cordia sulcata DC.

white manjack, mucilage manjack, *cereza blanca, mahot blanc*

Boraginaceae (borage family)

Unusually clean specimen of an open-grown tree with abundant flowers on the campus of the University of the Virgin Islands, St. Croix, in May. This tree was approximately 25 ft. (7.6 m) tall, and had a trunk diameter below the limbs of about 10 in. (25 cm).

White manjack is a very abundant small tree on St. Croix. Surprisingly, it is apparently rare or not found on the other V.I., but has been introduced into south Florida. On St. Croix, it always has flowers and fruit, even though it may lose its leaves in winter. It is identified by its (1) clusters of white to pale yellow flowers; (2) clusters of nearly round, whitish fruit; and (3) very coarse, gray-green leaves with toothed margins. *Cordia sulcata* is a member of a large family of mostly African species, but is native to St. Croix, and perhaps to some of the more easterly and southern West Indian islands.

Form. White manjack frequently has multiple trunks and can form dense thickets. Open-grown specimens with a single trunk to 8 in. (20 cm) in diameter can grow to 25 ft. (7.6 m) and have a spreading, rounded, dense crown.

Leaves and bark. Leaves are simple and alternate, dark green above, rough-hairy and gray below. They appear overall dull gray from a distance—probably in part because the rough upper surface retains dust. Leaves are 2–5 in. (5–13 cm) long and about 2 in. (5 cm) across. The bark is gray and fissured, and somewhat scaly.

Flowers occur terminally in many-branched, fragrant, erect clusters often 10 in. (25 cm) across. Individual flowers are stalkless, about 0.6 in. (1.5 cm) across. The noticeable part is the funnel-shaped, frilly, petal unit, with five prominent stamens.

Flowers were about 0.75 in. (2 cm) across.

Fruits are about 0.5 in. (1.3 cm) in diameter, on stalks about the same length. Inside the fruit is a mucilaginous pulp with a single seed.

Habitat. White manjack is found in dry coastal areas, often in poor soil. The tree prefers full sun, and is drought- and salt-tolerant.

Uses. The mucilage in the fruit has been used as glue and to help maintain hair dreadlocks. Parts of the tree have been used in various folk medicines, for example as a diuretic and to treat bronchitis. The light brown wood—lightweight, soft, and non-durable—finds few uses. Some consider white manjack to be an invasive nuisance on St. Croix, although it is sometimes planted for shade and hedging.

Fruit cluster and leaves in a tree; inset shows persisting dried fruit. Fruits were about 0.5 in. (1.3 cm) in diameter.

Crescentia cujete L.

calabash-tree, *higuera, arbol de las calabazas, calebasier*

Bignoniaceae (catalpa family)

A large open-grown tree on the grounds at Caneel
Bay resort, St. John, in November. This specimen
was about 22 ft. (7 m) tall, and about 20 in.
(50 cm) in diameter near the ground.

Calabash-tree is unusual-looking, It is native to the V.I. and has been widely
planted throughout the American tropics and elsewhere. The trees are almost
evergreen and are often laden with epiphytes, including orchids. Calabash-tree
is identified by its (1) unusual greenish-yellow to violet flowers which smell like
rotting cabbage, and which arise directly from the trunk and main branches;
(2) large gourdlike spherical or elliptical fruits; and (3) leaves, which arise
in clusters of 3–5 from short stubby spurs along the spindly main branches.
The popularity of the tree arises mainly because of its fruit, which, though
poisonous inside, has been used in many ways for centuries. It is common on
all the V.I., though perhaps less so on St. Thomas. It is a horticultural tree in
south Florida, but is not very common.

Form. Often having multiple trunks, calabash-tree branches near its base. The long, stout, mostly unbranched limbs create a tangled unkempt appearance because they criss-cross the center of the crown and then droop as the tree grows. The tree can become 30 ft. (9 m) tall and broad, and have a 12 in. (30 cm) or in some cases much larger trunk diameter at the base.

Leaf arrangement on a limb, with a flower bud, photographed in November on St. Croix. Longest leaf was about 4 in. (10 cm).

Leaves and bark. Although alternate, the leaves appear to be in whorls arising from spurs on the limbs. Leaves are 2–7 in. (5–18 cm) long. They are smooth-margined, dark green and shiny above, paler beneath. The petiole is short. The bark is slightly scaly on young trunks, becoming markedly fissured as the tree ages.

Flowers arise directly from limbs on short stalks. The tubular petal structure broadens out to about 2.5 in. (6.3 cm) in diameter, and is folded back on one side. Four stamens are prominent. Flowers are found intermittently throughout the year.

Open flower on limb in May, St. John. Length of flower, including its stem, was about 2.5 in. (6.3 cm).

Fruits grow to diameters of 5–12 in. (13–30 cm). When mature, they have thin, hard shells filled with a poisonous pulp containing many dark brown flattened non-poisonous seeds about 0.25 in. (0.6 cm) long. Fruits are found year-round.

Habitat. Most commonly found in drier areas, calabash-tree likes full sun and well-drained soils of various types. It is not salt-tolerant, but is highly drought-tolerant. It is probably resistant to high winds due to its open crown, small leaves, and strong wood.

Fruits on two different trees, both photographed on St. Croix in February; the spherical fruit was about 5 in. (12 cm) in diameter, and the elongated fruits were about 12 in. (30 cm) long.

Uses. The main use of this species is for production of its fruit, the shells of which have been used for everything from kitchen utensils to musical instruments (maracas among them), and the dried and ground seeds are used to make a sweet drink. The tree is also planted as an epiphyte host. The wood is hard and heavy, strong and flexible. It is light brown, and finds limited use in local woodworking, including boatbuilding, suggesting durability. The pulp contains a cyanide precursor, but has been used in folk medicines, for example as a purgative, and in treatment of urethritis, fever, and diseases of the respiratory tract, including bronchitis, whooping cough, epilepsy, and asthma. The stringy inner bark has been used to make rope and other cordage.

Note: Fruit pulp is poisonous.

Ficus citrifolia Mill.

shortleaf fig, wild banyan tree, *jagüey blanco, figuier maudit*

Moraceae (mulberry family)

Open-grown specimen by the Melvin Evans Highway *(thus the fence)* on St. Croix. This tree was at least 45 ft. (13.7 m) tall and had a trunk diameter, including the abundant aerial roots, of over 6 ft. (1.8 m).

Shortleaf fig is a common native evergreen tree in the V.I. and south Florida, frequently planted for its dense shade and attractive foliage. It shares in common with many other tropical figs bizarre aerial roots growing from the limbs, giving older trees a bearded look, and even obscuring the trunk. These vinelike aerial roots are aggressive and often strangle neighboring trees, making this species one of several "strangler figs." The tree is identified by its (1) aerial roots; (2) light gray, mostly smooth, bark; 3) the milky latex exuded from cuts through the bark; (4) prominent long-pointed leaf buds at the ends of twigs; (5) shiny, attractive leaves of variable lengths and widths; and (6) the year-round pairs of small, spherical, spotted fruits at leaf bases. It is native also to the Bahamas, Puerto Rico, and the rest of the West Indies.

Form. Usually shortleaf fig is a nicely shaped tree with a single trunk and very dense crown. Sometimes it develops several trunks from the aerial roots. The tree becomes 60 ft. (18 m) high and 2.5 ft. (76 cm) or more in trunk diameter.

Leaves and bark. Leaves are simple and alternate, and vary from 1.5–6 in. (4–15 cm) long and 0.75–3 in. (2–7.6 cm) across. The slender petioles are 0.75–2 in. (2–5 cm) long. Bark is relatively smooth, with many lenticels, but becomes fissured on older trunks.

Flowers occur inside the fruit, so are not visible. They are tiny, and are pollinated by a specific species of wasp.

Multi-stemmed tree formed by the aerial root habit. Masses of small aerial roots are seen hanging from the tree. The main trunk was about 16 in. (41 cm) in dbh. Inset shows bark with aerial roots. This striking specimen was photographed at the Marie Selby Botanical Gardens in Sarasota, Florida.

Fruits are about 0.4 in. (1 cm) in diameter, spotted with brownish patches, short-stalked, green becoming reddish-brown at maturity. They are usually in pairs at leaf bases. They are edible, but tasteless. Seeds are dispersed by birds, and often germinate on other plants; these young epiphytes send down aerial roots that eventually reach the soil and take root.

Habitat. Shortleaf fig likes full sun, and moist but well-drained soils. It is apparently moderately tolerant of salty air and drought.

Uses. Besides its ornamental uses (shade, appearance, amenity to being trimmed into hedges), shortleaf fig has light but strong wood that is used in construction over some of its range. The wood is, however, not at all durable. The tree is used as living fencing because cuttings sprout readily. Extracts of shortleaf fig have been used to treat wounds and infections.

Ficus elastica Roxb. Ex Hornem.

Indian-rubber fig, *palo de goma, arbre à caoutchouc*

Moraceae (mulberry family)

Open-grown, wide-spreading tree at La Reine, St. Croix. This tree was 35 ft. (10.7 m) tall, with a trunk diameter (including aerial roots) of about 5 ft. (1.5 m). The trunk itself was not visible (inset).

This is the common houseplant that is known simply as "rubber plant." In the V.I. and south Florida, though, it gets to be a fairly large tree, and in its native Indian jungles it grows to great size. Identification of this evergreen tree is easy, once one gets used to seeing such a big "houseplant." It is recognized by its (1) large, shiny, attractive leaves; (2) smooth light-gray bark; (3) copious white milky latex exuded by cuts through the bark; and (4) abundant aerial roots characteristic of *Ficus* spp.; and (5) long-pointed red-brown leaf buds at branch ends, and new reddish leaves. Although it is not especially abundant, it is found on all the major Virgin Islands as well as south Florida, and is easily spotted. The species does not reproduce by seed in the V.I. or south Florida, so has not become naturalized.

Form. Indian-rubber fig can become 60 ft. (18 m) tall or taller and 3 ft. (0.9 m) in trunk diameter. Its crown of dense foliage is wide-spreading (25–30 ft., 7.6–9 m, or more).

Leaves and bark. Leaves are alternate and simple, stiff and leathery, 4–12 in. (10–30 cm) long and 2–3 in. (5–7.5 cm) across, largest on young shoots.

Flowers. As with other *Ficus* species, flowers occur inside the fruit vessel, and are pollinated by a specific wasp. Both male and female flowers occur in the same vessel; they are tiny and numerous.

The largest leaves here were about 12 in. (30 cm) long.

Fruits are not plentiful in the V.I. or south Florida; none were found to photograph. They are about 0.5 in. (1.3 cm) in diameter, yellowish-green, occurring in pairs at leaf bases. When mature, they contain many tiny seeds and are edible. In other places, seeds are dispersed by birds, and often germinate on other plants; these young epiphytes send down aerial roots that often strangle their host.

Habitat. *Ficus elastica* can tolerate partial shade, is drought-resistant and moderately tolerant of salty air. It grows well on various types of well-drained soils. Its dense crown suggests low wind-resistance.

Uses. "Rubber plant" is a common houseplant all over the world. In tropical areas it is used as an ornamental—with due respect for its aggressive surface roots. The name comes from the fact that its latex was once the commercial source of rubber. It was replaced by an earlier-yielding Brazilian tree, *Hevea brasilensis*. The wood of Indian-rubber fig is light-colored and hard, but non-durable; it is not used in the V.I. or south Florida. Extracts of the plant reportedly have anti-inflamatory properties.

Hibiscus pernambucensis Arruda

seaside mahoe, sea hibiscus, *emajagua, majagua, bois flot, mahoe doux*

Malvaceae (mallow family)

Seaside mahoe tree forming a thicket along Queen Mary Highway on St. Croix; this thicket was approximately 45 ft. (14 m) high and more than 50 ft. (15 m) broad. Insets show base of the same tree, and bark.

The natural habitat of seaside mahoe is on the landward side of mangrove thickets. It is identified by its (1) tangled growth form; 2) nearly round, long-petioled, heart-shaped leaves, shiny green above and fuzzy gray-green below; (3) typical showy hibiscus flowers; and (4) gray-green fruit capsules, which turn brown when mature and split along 5 seams—and persist on the tree. Flowers and fruits can be found year-round in the V.I. and south Florida. Probably native to Brazil, *H. pernambucensis* has been planted widely and has become naturalized in south Florida and throughout the Caribbean. The species is very similar to *H. tiliaceous*, and was once classified as a variety of it.

Form. Seaside mahoe is a small tree to 40 ft. (12 m) high and with a trunk diameter 6 in. (15 cm) or more. The trunk usually branches near the ground. Limbs are long and flexible, often sagging to the ground, where new roots and stems form. This growth habit creates tangled and nearly pure thickets.

Leaves and bark. Leaves are simple and alternate, thin-textured, 4–7 in. (10–18 cm) in diameter, with 9–11 prominent veins curving out from the base, on petioles 2–5 in. (5–13 cm) long. The bark is relatively smooth, becoming fissured with age. Tough fibers in the inner bark give limbs the strength needed in the often harsh sites where the tree grows.

Morning and late afternoon flowers from the same tree. Flowers were about 2.5 in. (6.4 cm) across.

Flowers are funnel-shaped, about 3 in. (7.5 cm) long and broad, on whitish hairy stalks 1–2 in. (2.5–5 cm) long. Flowers begin the day pale yellow, but darken during the day to dark yellow, orange, and purple by nightfall. They bear both male and female organs.

Fruits are hairy, elliptic, pointed capsules about 1 in. (2.5 cm) long. Each of the 5 chambers has several reddish-black seeds about 0.14 in. (0.3 cm) long.

Habitat. *Hibiscus pernambucensis* is usually found in brackish, wet areas with poorly drained soil. It is also found on sandy sites occasionally, where its roots probably have access to water. It is drought-, wind-, and salt-tolerant and prefers full sun.

Mature, open fruits in crown; fruits were approximately 1.25 in. (3 cm) across.

Uses. Seaside mahoe is planted to control erosion, as a windbreak, and as an ornamental for its attractive flowers. Branches sprout readily, making the tree useful as living fence posts. The flowers and young leaves and inner bark are edible, although laxative properties have been ascribed to the leaves. The inner bark fibers have found use in cordage and woven goods. The wood is fairly soft, moderately heavy, and little used except for fuel. Sea hibiscus is attractive to hummingbirds and honeybees. Various *Hibiscus* spp. have been—and are being—studied for medical applications of the many diverse chemicals they produce, but the author found nothing specific about *H. pernambucensis*. However, it was found that decoctions made from roots, bark, flowers, and leaves of the closely related *H. tiliaceous* have been used to treat gastrointestinal ailments, constipation, cough, abscess, and hemorrhoids.

Hippomane mancinella L.

manchineel, manchioneel, death-apple, poison-guava, *manzanillo,*
maximilier

Euphorbiaceae (spurge family)

Manchineel tree about 42 ft. (6.7 m) tall and 11 in. (28 cm) in trunk diameter near the
base. This specimen was photographed near Manchineel Bay, St. Croix, in February.

This is the most toxic tree in the V.I. and south Florida, and perhaps all of the
American tropics. Stories of its poisoning and even killing people date from the
time of Columbus. Before that, Indians used its sap in making poison arrows. It
is evergreen, found along seashores, singly and in thickets, and is identified by
its (1) paired ever-present glossy yellow-green to pinkish, round, nearly stalkless
fruits to 1.5 in. (4 cm) in diameter; and (2) long-petioled, yellow-green leaves
with a raised dot (gland) on top at the midrib base, and rounded, small serrations
on the margins. When cut, the leaves, twigs, and fruit exude a caustic milky sap
best left untouched. Rainwater dripping through the crown causes skin blisters,
so this tree's shade is best avoided. Manchineel is native and common in the V.I.,
and is found throughout the West Indies, southern Florida, and the Florida Keys,
and on both the Atlantic and Pacific sides of Central America and tropical South
America.

Form. Manchineel attains heights of 40 ft (12 m) or more, and trunk diameters to 24 in. (61 cm). It usually has a single trunk and widely forking branches in a broad-spreading, fairly dense crown, except during the dry season (Dec. and Jan.), when the crowns thin. The trees often fall over and continue to grow in a prostrate position.

Inset shows a close-up of the diagnostic leaf gland.

Leaves and bark. The alternate, simple leaves in clusters at twig ends have leathery, waxy blades 2–4 in. (5–10 cm) long and up to about 2 in. (5 cm) across, with prominent yellow midribs. The dark brown or gray bark is thick and covered with small brown rounded lenticels; it becomes rough and scaly and/or fissured with age.

Flowers occur all year long, but are most abundant from spring to October; they are inconspicuous, grayish-green, in spike-shaped clusters. Male and female flowers are separate but on the same tree.

Fruits occur in pairs laterally on twigs. Each contains a thin apple-scented flesh surrounding a hard stone with 6–8 dark brown seeds about 0.25 in. (0.6 cm) long.

The stubby flower spike, here about 2 in. (5 cm) long, bears tiny yellow flowers.

Habitat. Manchineel is usually found growing in sandy and/or rocky soils near the sea. It is clearly salt-tolerant and resists drought and wind. It prefers full sun, but tolerates some shade.

Uses. Surprisingly, the wood of manchineel has been used in cabinetry, furniture, and construction. Care is taken in cutting the trees to avoid the sap, and the trees are usually girdled to let the sap dissipate before harvesting. The sapwood is yellowish and the heartwood dark brown. The wood is fairly hard, of medium weight, fairly strong, and takes a nice finish. The wood is durable except to drywood termites. Bees are attracted to the flowers, and the honey is non-toxic. Smoke from burning the fresh wood is quite irritating to skin, respiratory system, and eyes.

The deadly fruit is an attractive little "apple." These were about 1.25 in. (3 cm) in diameter.

Programs have attempted to eliminate this tree, but it spreads via seawater transport of its fruits, frustrating eradication efforts. Also, iguanas find the fruit non-toxic and eat it readily, spreading the seeds in their excrement. Some folk remedies have been prepared from parts of this tree and used to treat parasitic skin diseases, syphilis, tetanus, and various other ailments, and as a diuretic. Modern chemical studies have revealed that the caustic sap contains many different and interesting compounds.

Note: All parts of this tree are very toxic.

Hura crepitans L.

sandbox, monkey-no-climb-tree, hura, *molinillo, sablier*

Euphorbiaceae (spurge family)

Nicely shaped sandbox tree at St. George Village Botanical Garden, St. Croix. This tree was about 50 ft. (15 m) tall and 35 in. (89 cm) in dbh.

10 in.
25 cm

In a family with many poisonous plants, sandbox is no exception: its sap is caustic and very toxic. Even so, the tree is large and handsome, planted for its shade. It is readily identified from its (1) usually tall trunk with many stubby spines on the bark; (2) rounded dense crown; (3) elongated, heart-shaped, relatively large leaves, some of which have serrated margins; (4) bright red flower clusters (winter and spring); and (5) distinctive fruits. The tree is classified as deciduous, but some leaves seem to be present all year. Sandbox is native to the V.I. and to most of the rest of the West Indies as well as tropical America. It has been planted in south Florida and does well. *Hura crepitans* is common on St. Croix, and found but not as common on the other Virgin Islands or in south Florida.

Form. Sandbox can grow to over 100 ft. (30 m) tall, with trunk diameters of 24–48 in. (61–122 cm) or more. The bole can be as long as 75 ft. (23 m) before the first branch. In large trees, the crown frequently spreads to a diameter of 75 ft. (23 m) or more.

Leaves and bark. Leaf blades are 5–8 in. (13–20 cm) long and 4–5 in. (10–13 cm) across. Petioles are about as long as the blades. The bark is smooth except for the stubby spines.

Leaves on a twig. Lowest leaf was 13 in. (33 cm) long, including petiole.

Flowers. Male flowers occur on a long terminal stalk in dense elongated cylindrical clusters about 1–2 in. (2.5–5 cm) long and 0.75 in. (2 cm) in diameter. Female flowers occur on the same trees as males. They are single and lateral, near twig ends, and on stout short stalks 0.5–1 in. (1.3–2.5 cm) long.

Male flower cluster (left, about 1.25 in., 3 cm, long) and a female flower, slightly more than 1 in. (2.5 cm) long. Photos made by Jozef Keularts on St. Croix in May.

Fruits, green becoming brown, are capsules about 3 in. (7.6 cm) across, 1.5 in. (4 cm) high, on stout stems. They are grooved into 12 or more sections, each containing a single round flat brown seed up to 1 in. (2.5 cm) in diameter. When dry the woody capsule splits open violently with a loud crack, scattering the seeds up to 200 ft. (61 m).

Habitat. *Hura crepitans* is moderately drought-tolerant, and not especially salt-tolerant. It is probably not wind-resistant, and is found in moist non-coastal areas growing best in well-drained sandy loam soils. It prefers full sun but can tolerate some shade.

Uses. Sandbox is a pretty tree, and is planted in parks and along fences and roads. The wood is lightweight, and is not durable, but is used in general carpentry, for boxes, veneer, plywood, and other products. Lumberjacks must be cautious of the toxic and caustic latex, but the wood itself is not toxic. Folklore has it that the hollowed-out immature fruit capsules once were dried and used as ornamental containers for the fine sand used to blot ink, hence the name of the tree. Jewelry is made from the mature capsule sections. The seeds as well as the latex are toxic, and have been used to poison fish and other animals. Modern chemical studies have identified many compounds in the latex, many in common with manchineel latex. Despite their toxicity, the latex and decoctions of plant parts have been used in folk medicines to treat insect bites, abscess, trauma, rheumatism, headache, skin diseases, infections, and even leprosy.

Nearly mature fruit about to split open. Photo made in February on St. Croix.

Note: The latex of this tree is caustic and toxic.

Mangifera indica L.

mango, *mangó, manguier*

Anacardiaceae (cashew family)

Flowering mango in early February in west-central St. Croix; the tree was 42 ft. (13 m) tall and 28 in. (71 cm) in trunk diameter under the branches.

Mangoes are probably the most popular fruit from the tropics. The tree itself is relatively large and very handsome. Mango trees are recognized by their (1) dense, rounded crowns and stout trunks; (2) characteristic leaves, which are red when newly formed, and which are clustered at branch ends; and (3) flowers (Nov.–July) and fruits (May–Sept.). Also, cut twigs exude a white latex, and the cut trunk yields a resin. It is not surprising that mango, native to southern Asia, has been planted in tropical areas all over the world. It has been cultivated for over 1,000 years, has probably been in the V.I. since the late 1700s, was introduced into south Florida in the first half of the 1800s, and is now grown in large orchards. As with cashew, it is disconcerting to realize that mango is in the same family as poison ivy.

Form. *Mangifera indica* attains heights of 65 ft. (20 m) or more, with trunk diameters 36 in. (91 cm) or more. The evergreen crown may attain a diameter of 100 ft. (30 m).

Leaves and bark. Leaves are simple, closely alternate. Mature leaves are 6–14 in. (15–36 cm) long, dark green, and relatively shiny. The brown bark of young trees is smooth, with many thin fissures, but becomes rough and fissured with age.

Longest leaves were about 10 in. (25 cm).

Flowers in the hundreds are borne in erect, terminal branched clusters. Some of the tiny pink flowers are male and some bisexual, both kinds on the same tree. They are very fragrant and attract many bees.

Fruits vary greatly in color, size and shape, depending on the variety, from yellow to purple, 2.5–10 in. (6–25 cm) long, and from nearly spherical to kidney-shaped. They are almost always lopsided.

Flower clusters at branch ends; individual flowers (inset) were about 0.4 in. (1 cm) across.

Habitat. Mango prefers full sun, grows in a variety of soils, is resistant to wind, moderately so to salt and drought as long as it has plenty of rainfall during the summer months.

Uses. Many varieties of mango have been developed to improve the fruit, a very important article of commerce. India is the main producer, but many other areas grow mangoes commercially. They are common in U.S. grocery stores most of the year. The wood has wavy grain, is hard, fairly heavy, strong and has prominent pores. It has been much used in construction, even though it is not especially durable. An unusual use of mango in India was to make a light-resistant yellow dye used in oil painting—unusual because it is made from the urine of cows fed mango leaves. Many folk medicines have been prepared from mango extracts and resin, used in treating diarrhea, chronic dysentery, fever, chest problems, insomnia, diabetes, chronic urethritis resulting from gonorrhea, and other ills.

Nearly mature mangos of an elongated variety; these were about 7 in. (18 cm) long.

A word of caution: The sap of mango produces a poison ivy-like reaction in many people.

Beam of mango wood in an old Danish manor house built in about 1825, now part of the St. George Village Botanical Garden, St. Croix. The beam is approximately 12 in. (30 cm) deep and 8 in. (20 cm) wide.

Manilkara zapota (L.) van Royen

sapodilla, mespel, *chicle, níspero, sapodillier,* and many other local names

Sapotaceae (sapodilla family)

Open-grown sapodilla on U.S.D.A. grounds, Queen Mary Highway, St. Croix; the tree was about 40 ft. (12 m) tall and 14 in. (36 cm) in trunk diameter under the branches.

For many years, the latex of this tree was the source of the main ingredient of chewing gum. "Chicle" has now largely been replaced by a petroleum-derived rubber, but in the 1930s the U.S. imported over 10 millions pounds (4.5 million kg) per year. The handsome sapodilla tree is identified by its (1) sturdy trunk and dense evergreen crown; (2) attractive leaves clustered at branch ends; and (3) round tan fruits, which are present year-round in the V.I. and south Florida. A native of the Yucatan Peninsula (and debatably St. Croix), sapodilla has been planted nearly throughout the world's tropics for its edible fruit, shade, beauty—and chicle. It has been cultivated since ancient times in Mexico and surrounding areas, and has been in the V.I. and south Florida for many years. It is not especially common on the major Virgin Islands, being perhaps most abundant on St. Croix. It is considered to be invasive in south Florida.

Form. Sapodilla is an attractive, upright tree, its crown pyramidal when young, becoming round and broad when older. Open-grown trees reach 60 ft. (18 m) in height, but with forest competition forcing upward growth to reach sunlight, they may become over 100 ft. (30 m). Trunk diameters may reach 36 in. (91 cm).

Leaves and bark. The simple leaves are shiny, relatively dark green, and appear to be whorled but are actually alternate. Blades are 3–6 in. (7.5–15 cm) long or longer, with smooth margins. The bark is brown, deeply furrowed, and yields a white latex when cut through to the inner layers.

Leaves here varied from 3.5–6 in. (9–15 cm) in length.

Flowers are inconspicuous, greenish-yellow-brown, borne at leaf bases, and therefore at branch ends. They are bell-shaped and on brown hairy stalks about the same length as the flower—0.75 in. (2 cm).

Fruits are up to 4 in. (10 cm) in diameter, nearly spherical to somewhat flattened or elongated, depending on variety. They are covered by a thin sandpaper-textured rind that is green at first, becoming tan and smooth when ripe. The flesh is yellow to red-brown, coarse, and somewhat grainy, becoming soft and very juicy with a pearlike flavor when fully ripe. When immature, the fruit is astringent. Each fruit contains 1–5 black flattened seeds, easily removed from the mature fruit. Removing the seeds is important because they have a protruding hook that can lodge in the throat.

Opening flower buds; inset shows fully open flower. Note latex where leaves were removed.

Habitat. *Manilkara zapota* is very resistant to salt, drought, and wind, and survives in a variety of soils and habitats, including sea coasts. Its native soils are limestone-derived.

Immature fruit of about 3 in. (7.6 cm) in diameter; inset shows copious latex exuded by unripe fruit.

Uses. Once planted extensively for chicle production, sapodilla now is planted mainly as an ornamental and for fruit production, which is commercial in many tropical areas; sapodilla fruit is not yet common in U.S. markets. The ripe fruit is eaten raw with a spoon, as well as being made into jellies, preserves, etc. Sapodilla heartwood is dark red, hard, heavy, and durable. Locally it is used widely in construction and furniture-making and for a variety of other purposes. Intact sapodilla timbers have been found as support beams in Mayan temple ruins. The wood is not readily available in the U.S. As with most tropical trees, sapodilla extracts and concoctions have long been used in folk remedies, for example to treat diarrhea, hemorrhage, coughs, colds, bladder and kidney stones, insect bites, wounds, neuralgia, and high blood pressure.

Morinda citrifolia L.

painkiller, noni, Indian mulberry, *morinda, rhubarbe caraïbe*

Rubiaceae (madder family)

Small painkiller trees near Magens Bay, St. Thomas, in February; the taller one was about 13 ft. (4 m) high. Inset shows bark of a larger tree.

1 in.
2.5 cm

Painkiller (noni) fruit juice is one of the most popular botanical remedies and food supplements on the international market (see Uses below). *Morinda citrifolia* is a small evergreen tree, recognized by its (1) large, shiny and attractive leaves; (2) twigs that are square in cross section; and especially by (3) distinct fruit and flowers, which are present all year. It is native to tropical Australia, India, the East Indies, and Malaya, but has been planted in tropical regions all over the world. It readily becomes naturalized, as it has in the V.I. and south Florida, its seed being spread by bats and birds. It is common on St. Croix and Tortola, less so on the other islands; it is fairly common in the Florida Keys.

Form. Usually no taller than 20 ft. (6 m) with a 5-in. (13-cm) trunk diameter, and usually with a single trunk, painkiller often has a crooked, leaning form, especially when in a forest. The crown is moderately dense.

Leaves and bark. Leaves, with short petioles, are simple and alternate, 5–13 in. (13–33 cm) long, and have prominent veins and smooth margins. They have an undulating surface. The bark is slightly warty or scaly.

Leaves were about 10 in. (25 cm) long.

Flowers are borne in clusters on the surface of lateral ball-like heads on short stalks. The young flower heads (nascent fruits) are about 1 in. (2.5 cm) in diameter. Individual flowers are about 0.4 in. (1 cm) long and broad, white, with five waxy, pointed petal lobes. Flowers have both male and female parts.

A flower on the surface of a newly forming composite fruit. The flower was 0.4 in. (1 cm) across.

Fruits are actually composites of many individual ones, seen as four- to six-sided sections delineated on the overall composite surface. Each section has a rounded encircled dot at its center. The composite fruit—which is greenish-yellow, becoming white and soft at maturity—is irregular-shaped, roughly oblong, but usually bent, about 2.5 in. (6.4 cm) or more in maximum diameter. It has been likened to a scrubbed new white potato in appearance. It has an unpleasant cheeselike odor. It is edible, but eaten only when little else is available. Each fruit section contains two angled, flat seeds about 0.13 in. (3 mm) long.

This mature fruit was about 6 in. (15 cm) long.

Habitat. A hardy, often pioneer tree on poor sites, painkiller has a high tolerance for drought, salt, and various soils, including rocky ones and even sand. It can tolerate moderate shade and wind.

Uses. *Morinda citrifolia* is grown in plantations in Hawaii, Tahiti, and other locales to obtain the fruit juice, which is sold as is or as a dried powder. The list of ailments reportedly remedied by "noni juice," as well as extracts of the bark, leaves, and roots, is long indeed, accumulated over many years, especially in Asia. Included are treatments for arthritis, diabetes, ulcers, depression, and even cancer and AIDS. The name painkiller comes from use of the heated, wilted leaves to salve sore joints and swellings. Scientists have identified several bioactive chemicals made by the tree. A red fabric dye ("turkey red") has been obtained from the bark, and an orange dye from the roots. The tree is attractive, so is used as an ornamental in the V.I. and elsewhere. The wood is soft, light, non-durable, and little used.

Persea americana Mill.

avocado, alligator-pear, *aguacate, avocatier* (and many other names)

Lauraceae (laurel family)

Tree about 25 ft. (7.6 m) tall with a trunk diameter near the ground of 10 in. (25 cm), on the U.S.D.A. grounds off Queen Mary Highway, St. Croix, in November.

4 in.
10 cm

Familiar to all, avocado fruits are produced commercially in tropical and subtropical regions around the world. The tree is identified from its (1) flowers and/or fruit when present (much of the year); (2) fairly large, attractive leaves, clustered near branch ends; and (3) a slight anise odor of crushed leaves. The tree is native to tropical America, but not the V.I. or south Florida, where it has been widely planted. It is found but not especially common on all the major Virgin Islands; in south Florida, it is grown in large orchards and also used as a horticultural planting. It is also grown commercially in California.

Form. Trees may become 60 ft. (18 m) tall, with trunk diameters to 31 in. (79 cm). Unless pruned, as they are in orchards, the trees usually have a single trunk supporting a pyramidal, moderately dense crown with drooping branches.

Leaves and bark. Leaves are simple and alternate, glossy dark green above and dull below, with prominent veins and smooth margins. The blades are 4–8 in. (10–20 cm) long, with yellow-green petioles. Leaves are shed in early winter and reappear in late January, new ones often looking bright red for a while. Bark is brownish-gray, rough, and fissured on mature trees.

Longest leaves were about 7 in. (18 cm) long. Photo was taken in August in Gainesville, Florida, by Thomas Miller.

Flowers are bisexual, about 0.4 in. (1 cm) across, light green, with six pointed lobes. They occur near twig ends in clusters on short hairy stalks. In their profusion from January to May, they make the trees showy, and they emit a very pleasant odor attractive to bees.

Flower cluster in March, St. Croix; individual flowers (inset) were about 0.4 in. (1 cm) across.

Fruits hang on long stems near twig ends, usually in groups. Their weight makes the branches sag. They will not mature on the tree, and must be picked while still unripe. Shape varies, as does color—from green to yellow-green to red to almost black. Sizes vary from 3–16 in. (7.6–40 cm) long and up to 6 in. (15 cm) in diameter. They contain a single large seed.

Habitat. Avocado grows rapidly and flourishes in full sun on rich, well-drained soils on sites with adequate rainfall. However, the tree is drought-tolerant, moderately salt-tolerant, and will grow on a variety of soil types. It needs protection from high winds to avoid breakage.

Uses. *Persea americana* and related species are grown widely for their nutritious fruit,

These nearly mature fruits in the crown of a tree near the Marie Selby Botanical Gardens, Sarasota, Florida, in December, were about 5–6 in. (13–15 cm) long.

which is available nearly everywhere. The soft, butter-textured fruit pulp is high in oil, which is separated and used in a variety of specialty products such as soaps, lotions, and in aromatherapy. A brown dye is prepared from the seeds in Asia. The light-colored wood is soft and moderately heavy, non-durable, but easy to work and suitable for many products. Various parts of the tree are used in many folk remedies. The fruit skin and leaves have antibiotic properties, and leaf poultices have been applied to wounds. Leaf and fruit skin decoctions have also been employed to treat diarrhea, sore throat, hemorrhaging, and hepatitis, and as an abortifacient.

Terminalia catappa L.

Indian-almond, West Indian-almond, Pacific-almond, *almendra, amandier pays*

Combretaceae (combretum family)

Small trees on the campus of the University of the Virgin Islands, St. Thomas, in February.

The pagoda shape and presence of big red leaves make Indian-almond an attractive and interesting transplant from the East Indies. In south Florida and the V.I., it has become naturalized and is fairly common. The evergreen species is identified by its (1) large, leathery leaves, in clusters at branch ends; they turn red (or yellow or purplish) before falling, so that colored leaves are almost always present behind the shiny green ones; (2) horizontal branches in whorls or tiers at different levels on the trunk; and (3) ever-present flying saucer–shaped green fruits in clusters at branch ends. *Terminalia catappa* has been planted widely in the world's tropical regions, including south Florida, Hawaii, California, throughout the West Indies, and from Mexico to Peru and Brazil.

Form. Indian-almond attains heights to 55 ft. (17 m) and trunk diameters of 18 in. (76 cm) or more. The crown is of medium density and rounded. The branches are unusual in that they fork repeatedly into limbs of approximately equal length. The tree usually has a single trunk.

Leaves and bark. Leaves are 6–11 in. (15–28 cm) long and 3.5–6 in. (9–15 cm) across, with short, hairy petioles. They are simple and alternate. Veins are prominent, and margins are smooth. The smooth gray bark becomes fissured both vertically and horizontally with age.

Flowers occur in spike clusters 2–6 in. (5–15 cm) long. Individual flowers are star-shaped, only about 0.2 in. (0.5 cm) across, short-stalked or stalkless, and greenish-white. Bisexual flowers, as well as those of each sex separately, occur in the same clusters. They have only a slight odor to humans, but attract many bees.

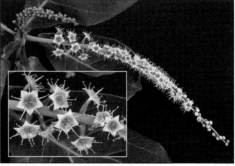

Flower spike, about 4 in. (10 cm) long, in November on St. Thomas; inset shows details of flowers, which were about 0.2 in. (0.5 cm) across.

Fruits are 2 in. (5 cm) or more long and 1 in. (2.5 cm) across, green turning red, yellow, or brown at maturity. At the side of each fruit is a curved spike longer than the fruit. The fleshy fibrous pulp surrounding the large seed is edible and very sweet when the fruits are very young, and the almond-shaped and -flavored seed is edible at maturity. The mature fruits float, which is probably responsible for the very wide natural distribution in the East Indies.

Habitat. Indian-almond is found in coastal areas, where it has a high tolerance for drought and salt; it is reasonably resistant to wind as well. It prefers full sun and well-drained soils and tolerates a variety of soil types, including sandy ones.

Fully expanded but still immature fruits. November, St. Thomas. Fruit was nearly 2 in. (5 cm) long.

Uses. Indian-almond is widely planted in tropical areas for its ornament, shade, edible nuts, and ability to stabilize soils. Its attractiveness as an ornamental is enhanced by its rapid growth. Other *Terminalia* species are grown for timber production, but *T. catappa* apparently is not, though it is used locally where durability is not important. Its wood is hard, moderately heavy, and moderately strong, and its heartwood is attractive. The bark, leaves, and especially the fruits have a high content of tannin, used in some areas to tan hides. Extracts of the leaves have been shown to have anti-diabetic and antioxidant activities. The many folk medicine uses include treatments for dysentery, gastric fever, diarrhea, skin rash, colds, asthma, high blood pressure, rheumatism, headache, and thrush. A black ink has been prepared from the fruits and bark, and a yellow-green dye from the leaves.

Thespesia populnea (L.) Sol. ex Correa

portiatree, *haiti-haiti, emajagüilla, catalpa*

Malvaceae (mallow, hibiscus, cotton family)

Typically formed tree on Magens Bay beach, St. Thomas, in February; this multi-stemmed tree was approximately 22 ft. (6.7 m) tall, with a basal diameter of about 16 in. (38 cm).

2 in.
5 cm

Portiatree is common in the V.I. and throughout the West Indies, as well as in south Florida—indeed the world's tropics in general. The small tree is identified by its (1) hibiscus-like flowers (almost always present), pale yellow becoming purple and shriveling within 24 hours; (2) persistent mature fruit—hard, dry, 5-sided and flattened; and 3) attractive, long-petioled, heart-shaped, dark green leaves. It is distinguished from seaside mahoe (*Hibiscus pernambucensis*), to which is related, by the heart-shaped rather than nearly round leaves. The fruit floats, accounting for the very wide distribution of portiatree. It is considered native to the V.I. and many other tropical areas, although not south Florida. There it was introduced in the early part of the last century, has become naturalized, and in fact is considered invasive in the Florida Keys.

Form. *Thespesia populnea*, in the wild, has a rather unruly form, with interlacing branches. The trees, reaching 30 ft. (9 m) high, often form tight thickets. When cultivated as an ornamental, this tree can easily be pruned to a pleasing form.

Leaves and bark. The simple and alternate leaves are fairly leathery, with petioles 2–4 in. (5–10 cm) long and blades 4–8 in. (10–20 cm) long. The gray bark is very rough and fissured.

The blade of the dominant leaf here was 6.25 in. (16 cm) long, with fruit diameters about 1 in. (2.5 cm).

Flowers, on stout stalks, are about 2 in. (5 cm) across and in length, with five overlapping petals.

Fruits are round and green when young, becoming brown and about 1.25 in. (3 cm) in diameter at maturity. They contain several angular seeds, but do not open, remaining on the tree for a considerable period before falling.

The delicate pale yellow flowers wilt and turn purple as the day progresses. Under the purple flower are nearly mature but still green fruits. Yellow flower was 2.25 in. (5.7 cm) across.

Habitat. This tree is very salt-tolerant, giving it an ecological edge by enabling it to grow along sandy beaches, where it is often found with seagrape. Portiatree prefers full sun, is very resistant to drought and wind, and grows in many types of soil, including sand and saturated sites at the edges of mangrove swamps.

Uses. *Thespesia populnea* is an attractive ornamental, useful in beach settings. It is also used as a street and park tree, and in living fences. The wood is attractive, with light- and dark-brown streaks, and is a valued timber in Hawaii. It is durable, even in the presence of drywood termites. It is valued for cabinetry, boat-building, and for turned objects, but the tree's small size limits its usefulness. Rope and other fiber products have been made from the tough inner bark.

The flowers and young leaves are eaten in some locales. Extracts of the fruit, leaves, and bark are used in folk medicines to treat, for example, lack of fertility, wounds, bacterial infections, mange, rash, itch, and rheumatism. Modern studies have identified the active chemicals and confirmed their value in some of these traditional uses.

Ziziphus mauritiana Lam.

India jujube, jujube, *aprín, pomme surette*

Rhamnaceae (buckthorn family)

This well-formed tree, near Cokley Bay on St. Croix in November, was 21 ft. (6.4 m) tall and each of two trunks was about 10 in. (25 cm) in dbh.

India jujube is a small evergreen tree that displays shiny green leaves with silvery-white undersides, very noticeable in the tropical breezes. The tree was introduced to tropical America from India and Southeast Asia for its edible fruit. It has escaped cultivation and is fairly common in some parts of the V.I. and south Florida. Identification is made by its (1) leaves, which, besides their striking green/white color, also have three prominent veins radiating out from the base; (2) small sharp spines on the twigs; (3) clusters of tiny pale yellow flowers (spring to fall) at leaf bases; and (4) copious round green fruits becoming orange-red when ripe in the winter, when the ground under the trees can be covered in a colorful carpet of slippery fruits.

Form. *Ziziphus mauritiana* is a compact tree, usually with a single trunk, up to 40 ft. (12 m.) high and 12 in. (30 cm) in trunk diameter. The rounded crown is dense, except it thins out during dry periods, when many of the leaves fall.

Leaves and bark. Leaves are simple and alternate, in two rows on zigzag twigs. They are 1.5–2.5 in. (4–6 cm) long and 1–1.75 in. (2.5–4.5 cm) wide. They have hairy petioles and very fine teeth on the margins. The brown bark is vertically fissured.

Flower clusters are numerous, less than 0.75 in. (2 cm) across, with individual flowers being only about 0.2 in. (0.5 cm) across.

Fruits are also numerous, 0.75–1 in. (2–2.5 cm) in diameter.

Habitat. *Ziziphus mauritiana* is found in coastal thickets and dry limestone forests. It has a high tolerance to salt, wind, and drought, and even to waterlogging. It prefers full sun and tolerates many soil types.

Uses. Sometimes used as an ornamental in the V.I. and south Florida, India jujube is cultivated as a valued fruit crop elsewhere, primarily in India. There, many varieties have been developed over many years, with improved taste, larger fruit, and pest resistance; some varieties are without thorns. The fruits are eaten raw, candied, prepared into drinks, and dried for use in chutneys. The wood—hard, tough, and attractive—is used to make furniture, tools, and many other products, as well as for fuel. An interesting use of the tree in India is as host to a lac-producing insect that coats the leaves with a resin—harvested to become the shellac of commerce. Leaves also are gathered as feed for silkworms. Many medicinal uses of the fruits, seeds, and leaves have been reported, including treatments for cuts and ulcers, fever, rheumatism, diarrhea, asthma, and gonorrhea.

Twig with leaves and both immature and nearly mature fruits. Note the thorns on the twig. Photographed in February on St. Croix.

Flowers in May on St. Croix.

LEAVES SIMPLE, OPPOSITE

Simple opposite leaves arise singly from the twig (or in some cases, directly from the trunk or branches), and are said to be opposite when the leaves are paired opposite one another. Five examples are shown here. The leaves of *Randia aculeata,* shown on the facing page, are tightly clustered, but in fact are opposite.

Rhizophora mangle (red mangrove)

Cassine xylocarpa (marbletree)

Pimenta racemosa (bay-rum-tree)

Clusia rosea (autograph-tree)

Randia aculeata (box-briar)

Avicennia germinans (L.) L.

black-mangrove, *mangle prieto, paletuvier*

Verbenaceae (verbena family)

Nicely formed tree on the south shore of central St. Croix, photographed in February; this tree was about 22 ft. (6.6 m) tall and 6 in. (15 cm) in trunk diameter at the base. Inset on right shows a thick patch of pneumatophores.

Black-mangrove is the hardiest of four mangroves in swampy areas in the V.I. and most of the Caribbean and Gulf coasts as well. It is identified by its: (1) numerous fleshy 2–12 in. (5–30 cm)-long pencil-like projections that arise vertically from horizontal roots in the mud; (2) opposite leaves on short petioles; (3) terminal clusters of small four-lobed white flowers; and (4) fleshy yellow-green, elliptical, flattened fruits. Flowers and fruit are found nearly year-round in the V.I. and in south Florida. The species is native to and fairly common on all the Virgin Islands and in south Florida.

Form. *A. germinans* is a small evergreen tree up to 40 ft. (12 m) tall, with trunk diameters to 12 in. (30 cm). It occurs growing together with the other mangroves. It has a rounded, fairly dense crown with spreading branches. Large trees may have root masses to 1.5 ft. (0.5 m) long hanging in the air from upper parts of their trunks. The pencil-like projections (pneumatophores) under the trees apparently supply oxygen to the roots.

Leaves, flower, and buds, photographed in the V.I. in April.

Leaves and bark. Leaves are 2–4.5 in. (5–11 cm) long and 0.5–0.75 in. (1.3–1.9 cm) broad. Upper surfaces are yellow-green, often shiny, whereas the lower surfaces are gray-green and hairy. Both surfaces often have scattered salt crystals resulting from excretion of salt solutions by the leaves. The bark is smooth and dark gray or brown, becoming fissured, scaly, and almost black with age.

Flower clusters, about 1 in. (2.5 cm) in diameter, are made up of stalkless white flowers, each about 0.4 in. (1 cm) across.

Fruits, when mature, are about 1 in. (2.5 cm) long. Each fruit contains one dark green seed, often seen germinating on the tree, splitting the seed coat. When it falls, the young plant continues to grow in place, or grows after being carried by currents to other locales where the young plant takes root.

Habitat. Black-mangrove is part of swamp forests occurring at sea level and in brackish water along silty shores. It prefers full sun but can tolerate some shade, and is very salt-, and probably wind-tolerant.

Fruit was about 1 in. (2.5 cm) long. Mature fruit in November.

Uses. Ecologically, black-mangrove, together with the other mangroves, is very important in preventing erosion and soil loss. The resin is or has been used to treat various ailments, including diarrhea, dysentery, hemorrhoids, wounds, and even cancers. The wood is heavy, difficult to work, and little used. Flowers are attractive to bees and important in honey production.

Note: The raw fruits are toxic, but become edible when cooked.

Calophyllum antillanum Britton

galba, Antilles calophyllum, false mamey, *maría, santa-maría, galba odorant*

Clusiaceae (mammee-apple family)

Small galba tree, 26 ft. (8 m) tall and 19 in. (49 cm) in dbh, on the campus of the University of the Virgin Islands, St. Croix, in February.

The genus name means "beautiful leaf," and galba does have beautiful leaves. Native to the Virgin Islands and Greater Antilles, galba has been planted widely throughout the Caribbean and in other parts of the American tropics. It is one of the few native West Indian species widely used for timber. It is identified by its (1) leaves, red when they first emerge, becoming dark green and leathery; (2) dense, spreading evergreen crown; (3) (spring and summer) fragrant white flowers with yellow centers; (4) (spring to winter) nearly spherical fruits, green becoming light brown and eventually wrinkled; and (5) pale yellow latex exuded by cut stems. Galba is found throughout tropical America; several varieties have been classified as different species by some authors, but the V.I. variety seems to be unique. It is found but not especially common on the major Virgin Islands. It is not planted in south Florida, but specimens can be seen at Fairchild Tropical Botanic Garden, Coral Gables. (This species is synonymous with *C. calaba*.)

Form. Galba usually has a single trunk. It can become 100–150 ft. (30–45 m) tall and 6 ft. (183 cm) in diameter on the most favorable sites. In the V.I., specimens up to about 75 ft. (23 m) tall and 1.5 ft. (46 cm) in diameter have been noted.

Leaves are opposite, 2.5–5 in. (6–12 cm) long and 1.25–2.5 in. (3–6 cm) across, with distinctive fine parallel veins only about 0.03 in. (0.8 mm) apart and nearly perpendicular to the midribs.

Flowers. Individual flowers are up to 1.0 in. (2.5 cm) across. The flower stem clusters are borne laterally, usually arising in the leaf bases. They are up to 5 in. (13 cm) long. Male and bisexual flowers are borne on the same tree; there are no female-only flowers.

Fruits, about 1.5 in. (4 cm) in diameter, contain a single large, rounded seed. When mature, the skin is rumpled, hard, and dry. It is waterproof, allowing the fruits to float and be carried by water.

Largest leaf was about 6 in. (15 cm) long. Inset shows close-up of the (male) flowers. Photographed in February.

Habitat. Galba grows on most sites, in most soils, and tolerates degraded sites. It is very salt-tolerant, prefers full sun, and can tolerate moderate drought.

Uses. *Calophyllum antillanum* has many past and present uses, from folk medicines to ornamental plantings. The fruit is not eaten by humans because of its pungent flavor, but is fed to pigs. Easily established from seeds, galba is used for its dense shade and beauty, for reclaiming degraded soil, and as a windbreak, especially where salt-tolerance is important. It is grown for commercial timber production on some of the West Indian islands and other parts of the American tropics. The wood is strong, of average density, and has an attractive grain. It is moderately durable, and although difficult to season, is widely used in the American tropics for general construction, flooring, furniture, boatbuilding, and a variety of other products. Galba seed oil has been used in lamps. Extracts of various galba tissues have been used to treat skin diseases, high blood pressure, abcesses, hernia, and burns. Ongoing pharmacological research has identified specific compounds in galba extracts and is assessing their medical and other uses.

Nearly mature fruit cluster in tree; February.

Immature and mature fruit; February.

Cassine xylocarpa Vent.

marbletree, poisontree, *coscorrón, bois tan*

Celastraceae (bittersweet family)

Cassine xylocarpa trees are numerous at Magens Bay beach on
St. Thomas; this tree, photographed in May, was about 20 ft.
(6 m) tall and 6 in. (15 cm) in dbh.

Marbletree is a common beach tree in the V.I., and is also found in rocky areas,
sometimes growing out of rock crevices. This small evergreen tree is recognized
by its (1) attractive leaves, which are mostly opposite, but sometimes alternate;
(2) clusters of small flowers, usually present; (3) greenish-yellow, round, very hard,
woody fruits, also usually present. It is native to the V.I. and the American tropics,
being found from Mexico to Venezuela, the Lesser Antilles through Martinique
and St. Vincent and the Grenadines. In the V.I., it is found but uncommon on
St. Croix and common on the other islands. It has been introduced into south
Florida, where specimens can be seen, among other places, at Fairchild Tropical
Botanic Garden, Coral Gables.

Form. *Cassine xylocarpa*, though slow-growing, can attain heights of 35 ft. (11 m) and trunk diameters of 8 in. (20 cm). It is usually an attractive tree with a dense crown. It frequently has multiple stems arising from the root crown or low on the trunk.

Leaves vary greatly in size, from 1–4 in. (2.5–10 cm) in length and proportionally wide; they can, however, be larger or smaller depending on site.

Flowers are tiny and occur in clusters 0.4–1.25 in. (1–3 cm) across at leaf bases.

Fruits are 0.75–1.25 in. (2–3 cm) in diameter.

Habitat. Marbletree is found in coastal dry as well as moist habitats. It usually grows on well-drained sites, and is very drought-tolerant. It is also salt-tolerant, often being found near the sea. It prefers full sun.

Uses. *Cassine xylocarpa* is attractive enough to be a landscape tree, but apparently is not used widely, perhaps because of its slow growth rate. It does serve to shelter and feed various types of wildlife in harsh seaside environments. Interestingly, the plant is an excellent accumulator of the element nickel from the soil, which means it might have use in removing this toxic element from contaminated sites. Stimulants have been prepared from the fruits and other plant parts.

Largest leaves were about 2.5 in. (6 cm) long. Photographed in January.

Flower and flower buds in a cluster in May; flower was about 0.2 in. (0.5 cm) across.

Fruit cluster on twig in February. Each fruit was about 1 in. (2.5 cm) long.

Clusia rosea Jacq.

autograph-tree, Scotch attorney, pitch-apple, wild mammee, *cupey, figuier maudit*

Clusiaceae (mammee-apple family)

Small, nicely formed tree on the campus of the University of the Virgin Islands, St. Croix. This tree, photographed in May, was approximately 18 ft. (5.5 m) high and 10 in. (25 cm) in trunk diameter below the branches.

Autograph-tree, like the figs (*Ficus* spp.) is attractive, but also like figs has a dark side: it strangles other trees. *Clusia rosea* is evergreen, recognized by its (1) thick, leathery, shiny leaves; (2) spreading, dense crown; (3) large, showy white flowers, developing nearly year-round from pink-tinged terminal buds; and (4) round fruits, yellow-green, becoming brown and splitting open into 7–9 sections at maturity. The name "autograph-tree" comes from the persistence of scratched writing or other marks on the long-lived leaves. Like the strangler figs,

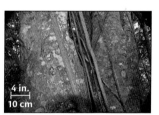

Bark and aerial roots of a much larger tree in the hills of St. John.

autograph-tree often begins life as an epiphyte, with seeds germinating in the fork of another tree, and the new plant sending down numerous aerial roots that eventually strangle their host. It is native to the West Indies and south Florida, and from tropical Mexico down into northern South America.

Form. Autograph-tree can have single or multiple trunks, and can be pruned readily to the desired number in landscaping applications. The crown is spreading, rounded, and very dense, with limbs drooping with the weight of the leaves and fruit. *Clusia rosea* can attain heights of 60 ft. (18 m) and trunk diameters of 24 in. (61 cm). In the V.I., one frequently sees autograph-trees along roadsides sticking out from the forest.

Leaves and bark. Leaves are opposite, 3–6 in. (7.6–15 cm) long and 2–4.5 in. (5–11 cm) across. The gray-brown bark is fairly smooth, but somewhat warty.

These leaves were 5–6 in. (13–15 cm) long.

Flowers occur one to three at branch ends, on short downward-curving stalks. The noticeable feature is the fleshy 3 in. (7.6 cm)-diameter arrangement of 6–8 white concave petals; these are notched at the apex. Male and female flowers occur on separate trees, with the former differing by having a sticky yellow ring of fused stamens at the center.

Flower and unopened bud in crown, photographed in February; the (male) flower was about 2 in. (5 cm) in diameter.

Fruits are eaten by birds and bats, spreading the seeds. Each fruit capsule contains an orange-red pulp with many 0.2-in. (0.5 cm)-long seeds. The capsule splits open into a 7–9-pointed star shape when mature.

Habitat. Autograph-tree is one of the most habitat-tolerant trees in the V.I. and south Florida. It grows in deep shade and open sun, in various soils, and is very resistant to drought, salt, and wind.

Uses. Because of its ease of cultivation in many kinds of habitats, and the attractiveness of its rich foliage, *Clusia rosea* is valued as an ornamental. The fruit and bark latex hardens on contact with air and has been found helpful in sealing boat seams, as plaster in folk medicine, and for other uses. Extracts of the fruit and bark have served to treat leg ulcers and to prevent infection. Modern studies show the promise of *Clusia rosea* fruit chemicals as anti-tumor agents.

Open fruit in crown, with seeds missing; the red material surrounded the seeds, which birds eat so quickly they are almost impossible to find. Fruit diameter about 1.5 in. (4 cm). Photographed in February on St. John.

Eugenia uniflora L.

Surinam-cherry, Cayenne-cherry, Florida-cherry, *cereza de Cayena, petanga, cerise de Cayenne*

Myrtaceae (myrtle family)

Multi-stemmed, bushy specimen in a fruit orchard in central St. Croix, about 12 ft. (3.7 m) tall. Inset shows bark of a much larger, hurricane-damaged tree in the Fruit and Spice Park, Homestead, Florida.

Surinam-cherry is one of several species of *Eugenia* in the V.I. and south Florida. Most are bushes, but some, including *E. uniflora*, become small trees. It is identified by its (1) simple, opposite, dark green leaves with short petioles; (2) (spring) small white flowers on long slender stalks and with long stamens; (3) (summer into fall) colorful, ribbed fruit on long stems; and (4) flaking, mottled bark typical of the Myrtaceae. It is native to Surinam and other parts of South and Central America, and has been planted widely in tropical and subtropical areas of the world. Found on all of the major Virgin Islands, it is not especially common despite having escaped cultivation. In south Florida it has escaped and earned itself a reputation as a nuisance species.

Note: The several other species of *Eugenia* that become tree-size in the V.I. and south Florida often have "stopper" in their common names. They share the simple, opposite leaves, the "myrtle" bark, and the delicate stamen-dominated flowers with *E. uniflora*.

Form. *Eugenia uniflora* can grow to a height of 25 ft. (7.6 m) and trunk diameters of 6 in. (15 cm) or more. It has spreading, slender branches, some protruding from the medium-density crown. It is usually encountered as a multi-stemmed bush.

Leaves and bark. Young leaves are bronze or red-colored, becoming glossy and dark green as they mature. The leaves smell resinous. The bark is relatively smooth, tan to light gray.

Flowers are borne 1–4 from leaf bases. They are about 0.4 in. (1 cm) across the four white petals. Fifty to sixty stamens with yellow tips protrude about 0.4 in. (1 cm) from the centers of the flowers.

The largest fruit here was about 1 in. (2.5 cm) in diameter.

Fruits are 0.75–1.5 in. (2–4 cm) in diameter, shorter than wide, with 7 or 8 ribs. They turn from green to yellow to orange to bright red as they mature. One variety has purple fruit when mature. The edible, delicious fruits are sweet and slightly tangy, with an underlying resinous flavor. Each contains 1–3 seeds with one flattened side.

Habitat. Surinam-cherry tolerates a variety of types of soil, prefers full sun, is drought-tolerant but not salt-tolerant. It does not resist high winds.

Uses. *Eugenia uniflora* is widely used as a hedge plant in central and south Florida. It responds well to pruning, and its new red leaves add to its

0.5 in.
1.3 cm

attractiveness. It is not grown widely for its fruit in the V.I. or south Florida, but is grown as a market crop in Brazil and probably elsewhere. Leaf extracts are used in South America to stimulate appetite, to aid digestion, and to treat fever and colds.

Guapira fragrans (Dum. Cours.) Little

black mampoo, beefwood, *corcho, mapoo*

Nyctaginaceae (four-o'clock family)

Well-formed, open-grown specimen on the grounds of Caneel Bay resort, St. John. This tree was 32 ft. (9.8 m) tall and 16 in. (41 cm) in dbh.

One of the most common trees on the major Virgin Islands, black mampoo is native. It is not reported from south Florida. This attractive evergreen tree is identified by its (1) simple and opposite leaves, with short yellow-green petioles, and frequently with insect galls on older leaves; (2) twigs that are yellow-green when young, becoming gray with age; (3) numerous rounded, dark bark lenticels; (4) flowers (spring and summer), which are in branched pale green clusters; and (5) little elongated olive-shaped fruits, red turning black (spring and summer; on female trees only). *Guapira fragrans* is found through the West Indies except the Bahamas, and in northern South America.

Form. Black mampoo is a small- to medium-size tree to 40 ft. (12 m) tall and 20 in. (51 cm) trunk diameter, with a nicely rounded crown when open-grown. The tree usually has a single bole that branches several feet off the ground.

Leaves and bark. Leaves are 2–6 in. (5–15 cm) long and 1–2.5 in. (2.5–6.3 cm) across. The mostly gray bark is relatively smooth except for the lenticels, and small fissures that develop with age.

Flowers occur mostly at twig ends in branched clusters that are 3–4 in. (7.5–10 cm) long and 1.5–3 in. (4–7.5 cm) broad. Flowers themselves are small, tubular, and yellow-green, with protruding stamens (males); they are only slightly fragrant (despite the tree's specific epithet).

Fruits are fleshy and occur in clusters that are up to 4 in. (10 cm) long and 3 in. (7.5 cm) across. Each is up to 0.5 in. (1.3 cm) long, on a stalk, and has one hard seed.

Male flower cluster.

Habitat. In the V.I., black mampoo is found in both the dry forest ecosystem and in moist regions. Because it is found near the sea, it obviously resists salty air and wind. It prefers full sun, but is found also as an understory tree. It is drought-tolerant and grows in various soil types.

Uses. Black mampoo is used as a landscape tree in open areas near the sea, where it is attractive, with its single upright trunk and dense rounded crown. Otherwise, the tree is little used. The wood is light, soft, and non-durable, with little fuel value. No references to the tree's use in folk medicines were found.

Immature and mature fruit clusters.

Laguncularia racemosa (L.) Gaertn. F.

white-mangrove, mangel, white buttonwood, *mangle blanco, mangle blanc*

Combretaceae (combretum family)

Sizeable specimen at the Stouffer-Vinoy Golf Course, St. Petersburg, Florida. This tree, photographed in December, was 34 ft. (10 m) tall and about 8 in. (20 cm) in dbh.

One of four mangrove tree species in the V.I. and south Florida, white-mangrove is probably the most common. This rapidly growing small evergreen tree is identified from its (1) location on the landward side of mangrove communities; (2) opposite, somewhat fleshy, dull yellow-green leaves with two raised glands at the leaf base; and (3) flowers and fruit, which are present almost year-round. The species is native to the West Indies, tropical continental America, south Florida, and is also found in tropical West Africa. It is found along both coasts of Florida up to about 29° north.

Form. *Laguncularia racemosa* grows to 40 ft. (12 m) or more and 12 in. (30 cm) in trunk diameter. Often it has multiple trunks. The crown is fairly dense and spreading.

Leaves and bark. Leaves are simple, smooth-margined, 1.5–4 in. (4–10 cm) long, with short reddish petioles. The bark is gray-brown, rough, and fissured.

Flowers occur in terminal or lateral branched clusters 1–4 in. (2.5–10 cm) long. Individual flowers are greenish-white, bell-shaped, and about 0.2 in. (0.5 cm) long. They are most numerous in spring.

Fruits, like the flowers, occur in clusters. Individual fruits are velvety, flattened, ridged, and vase-shaped, with a liplike extension at the end. They are gray-green, becoming brown. Each individual fruit is about 0.75 in. (2 cm) long and contains a single seed. The fruits float and often germinate in the water that disseminates them.

Leaves and flower clusters in April in south Florida; insets show close-up of flowers and diagnostic leaf glands.

Habitat. White-mangrove grows in saturated soils of a variety of types. It prefers full sun and is very salt- and wind-tolerant.

Uses. The bark and leaves are rich in tannin that is used commercially in some locations, including Brazil, to tan hides. The tannin is also used in local medicines to treat mouth ulcers, fever, and scurvy. Anti-tumor activity has also been reported for the tannin.

Fruit cluster, photographed in May in south Florida.

Plant extracts are said to be a tonic and useful in treating dysentery. The brown to yellow-brown wood is hard and heavy but not durable. Locally it has a variety of uses, from tool handles to charcoal, but the trees are too small for extensive use in construction.

Mammea americana L.

mammee, mammey-apple, *mamey, abricotier d'Amérique*

Clusiaceae (mammee-apple family)

Nicely formed open-grown tree, approximately 40 ft. (12 m) tall with a 13 in. (33 cm) dbh, on the grounds of the Lawaetz Museum on St. Croix.

2 in.
5 cm

With its dark green, large and shiny leaves, this beautiful evergreen tree resembles the southern magnolia of North America. It is identified by its (1) opposite leaves, which are up to 8 in. (20 cm) long; (2) white flowers with large rounded yellow centers (spring to fall); (3) round fruit present year-round; and (4) the pale yellow latex exuded by cut inner bark. Mammee is native to the West Indies and has been widely planted in many tropical areas. It is found but not common in the V.I.— probably more so on St. Croix than the other islands. It was introduced into south Florida early in the last century, but is not widespread; specimens are found at Fairchild Tropical Botanic Garden in Coral Gables, and south through the Keys.

Form. A stout, erect trunk supports sturdy, upward-reaching branches and a dense pyramidal crown of foliage. The tree can reach 65 ft. (20 m) or more in height and 24 in. (61 cm) or more in trunk diameter.

Leaves and bark. Leaves are leathery and glossy on the upper surface. They have many parallel straight veins running from the midrib to the smooth edges. The somewhat mottled red-brown bark is rough on older trees.

Flowers are not easy to see, being hidden in the foliage. They are about 2 in. (5 cm) across, with 4–6 overlapping waxy petals. The petals turn back with age.

Fruit. The edible fruit is nearly spherical, 4–10 in. (10–25 cm) in diameter and with a short stout stalk and thick gray-brown rind. It is hard until fully ripe. Imbedded in the center are 1–4 rough seeds about 2 in. (5 cm) long; these are toxic, and the flesh next to them is bitter.

Habitat. *Mammea americana* prefers deep, rich well-drained soils, but is fairly tolerant of various sites. It is not especially salt- or drought-tolerant, so is not found very near the sea or in dry areas. The tree prefers full sun or bright partial shade.

Flowers and buds in tree; flower centers were about 0.75 in. (2 cm) across.

Uses. The fruit of mammee is tasty, and is eaten in the V.I. and elsewhere. The fruit is sold at roadside stands, and is eaten raw or made into juice, jam, chutney, etc. Some people reportedly get a stomachache from eating the raw fruit. The fruit has potential for commercial development, but apparently no one has taken the initiative to research its harvest, storage, transportation, etc. Mammee is planted as an ornamental for its shade and beauty, as well as its fruit. The sapwood is light brown and the heartwood a deep reddish-brown, resembling heart mahogany. It is not easy to dry without developing defects, but once dry it works well and takes a fine polish. It is used locally in furniture-making, general construction, and for fence posts and other items. It is fairly decay-resistant, but is not resistant to termites. The toxic seeds and other plant parts have been used to prepare broad–spectrum insecticides. The resin and other plant parts have also been used in folk medicines, especially to treat parasitic skin diseases, eczema, worms, and lice, and to reduce malarial fever when quinine fails.

Note: Seeds are toxic.

Myrciaria floribunda (West ex Wild.) Berg.

guavaberry, rumberry, *mirto, cococarette*

Myrtaceae (myrtle family)

Open-grown specimen on the Lawaetz Museum grounds on St. Croix, approximately 25 ft. (7.6 m) tall; the trunk was 6 in. (15 cm) in diameter below the limbs.

This attractive evergreen tree produces the guavaberries of V.I. guavaberry liqueur fame. It is identified by its (1) simple and opposite, lance-shaped and long-pointed leaves, very aromatic when crushed; (2) round clusters of small white flowers at leaf bases (late spring and summer); (3) small stalkless fragrant round, red or yellow fruits scattered along stems, maturing in summer and fall; and (4) flaking, mottled bark. Guavaberry is widespread in many parts of the American tropics, throughout the West Indies, in tropical Mexico, Central America down to Peru, and to eastern Brazil. It is native to the V.I., and is common on St. John and Tortola but less common on the other islands. Guavaberry is apparently rare in south Florida; Fairchild Tropical Botanic Garden in Coral Gables lists several specimens in its collection.

Form. *Myrciaria floribunda* attains heights of 55 ft. (17 m) and trunk diameters of 12 in. (30 cm). It often branches near the ground into several upright stems that support a dense crown.

Leaves and bark. Leaves are smooth-margined, 1–3.5 in. (2.5–9 cm) long and 0.5–1.5 in. (1.3–4 cm) wide, with short petioles. The bark is relatively smooth, tan to light gray, flaking off in plates to reveal a lighter-colored underlayer (as seen with other Myrtaceae trees).

Flowers. Individual flowers in their clusters are tiny, with four frilly petals and numerous yellow-tipped, protruding stamens.

Fruits are about 0.5 in. (1.3 cm) in diameter, nearly globose. The orange flesh is strongly aromatic, edible, and surrounds a single round seed (sometimes two).

Habitat. Guavaberry grows on both moist and dry sites in various types of soil, but prefers rich loam. It also prefers full sun and is drought-resistant and moderately wind- and salt-tolerant.

Uses. Guavaberry makes an attractive street and yard ornamental, for which it is planted in the V.I. The "berries" are eaten off the tree in many places and are used to produce juice, jellies, and jams. They are also used commercially to make guavaberry liqueur, which is readily available in the V.I. In some locales the fruits are sold for use in making a purifying syrup and for treating liver ailments.

New leaves are red; older leaves were about 1.25 in. (3 cm) long.

1 in.
2.5 cm

Cluster of flowers, with inset showing close-up.

Mature black guavaberries in a crown; immature green and red ones are also present. Photograph taken by Dale Morton on St. Thomas.

Pimenta racemosa (Mill.) J. W. Moore

bay-rum-tree, wild cilliment, wild cinnamon, cinnamon, *malagueta, bois d'Inde* (and many others)

Myrtaceae (myrtle family)

Tall roadside specimen near Cinnamon Bay, St. John, in March. This tree was over 40 ft (12 m) in height and about 9 in. (23 cm) in dbh.

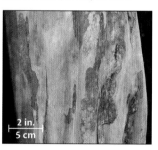

In the late 1800s and early 1900s, bay-rum-tree was grown extensively on St. John for the production of its aromatic leaf oil. The tree is identified by its (1) opposite, smooth-margined, dark green leaves, which when crushed have a strong bay rum (clove/cinnamon) fragrance; (2) smooth, gray to light brown bark, which peels off in strips and patches to reveal lighter shades of underlayer; (3) delicate white, very fragrant flowers (April–Aug.), which are borne in rounded clusters; and (4) small round/elongated fruits (summer–fall), green turning black at maturity. Bay-rum-tree is native to Puerto Rico and perhaps to the V.I. and the other West Indian islands as well, and has been planted widely elsewhere. The tree is fairly common on St. John, but not on the other major Virgin Islands or in south Florida. In 2006 Fairchild Tropical Botanic Garden of Coral Gables recommended this tree for horticultural planting in the Miami area.

Form. Bay-rum-tree is usually erect, attaining heights of 40 ft. (12 m) or more and trunk diameters of 8 in. (20 cm) or more. The crown is evergreen and columnar or pyramidal in shape. The trunk is slightly fluted.

Leaves and bark. The simple leaves are stiff, 1.25–4 in. (3.2–10 cm) long or longer. Twigs are almost square in cross section. Very young leaves frequently have a red hue. Bark on older trees may become slightly rough and somewhat fissured.

Flowers are borne in branching clusters, 1–3 in. (2.5–7.5 cm) across, which occur both laterally and terminally. The ball-shaped buds are white. Individual flowers are borne on short stalks, and are about 0.5 in. (1.3 cm) across. From their centers extend numerous white stamens. The flowers are bisexual.

Largest leaf here was about 5 in. (13 cm) long.

Fruits are borne in branching clusters, 1–3 in. (2.5–7.5 cm) across, which occur both laterally and terminally. Individual flowers are borne on short stalks, and are about 0.5 in. (1.3 cm) across. From their centers extend numerous white stamens.

Habitat. *Pimenta racemosa* grows best in full sun or light shade on sheltered sites in well-drained soils. It is moderately drought-, salt-, and wind-tolerant.

Uses. The tree is still cultivated for its oil, which is produced commercially at least on the Caribbean island of Dominica. Several varieties of bay-rum-tree are recognized, some of which are better oil-producers than others. The oil is used in cosmetics, and the oil and extracts of leaves and other plant parts are used in local medicines to treat toothache, sore throat, colds, pneumonia, diarrhea, rheumatism, incontinence, stroke, and for their anti-inflammatory and analgesic properties. Bay-rum-tree wood finds uses locally where resistance to dry wood termites is needed, as in fence posts.

Flower cluster, with inset showing close-up of flower. Photographed in June on St. Croix by Jozef Keularts.

Immature and one mature fruit among leaves. Photographed in July on St. Croix by Jozef Keularts.

Pisonia subcordata Sw.

water mampoo, mampoo, loblolly, *corcho blanco, mapou gris*

Nyctaginaceae (4-o'clock family)

Open-grown tree on the campus of the University of the Virgin Islands, St. Thomas, in May. This tree was over 45 ft. (13.7 m) tall and over 36 in. (91 cm) in diameter at its swollen base.

4 in.
10 cm

Water mampoo is one of the most common trees in dry, rocky eastern forests of the V.I.; often it is the largest tree. It is identified by its (1) large, shiny, nearly round, opposite leaves; (2) swollen, misshapen base with exposed roots; (3) clusters of small green-white flowers (late winter into summer), which occur in branching long-stemmed clusters; and (4) clusters of elongated, ridged fruits. The spongy tissue making up the swollen trunks of these trees stores water, allowing this species to survive severe droughts. Water mampoo is a native of the V.I. and the West Indies in general. *Pisonia rotundata*, found in the Florida Keys, is listed as synonomous with *P. subcordata* by University of Florida experts.

Form. This tree often has multiple, gnarled trunks. It is a medium-size tree to 50 ft. (15 m) tall and 24–36 in. (61–91 cm) in trunk diameter. Branches and twigs are stout, and the rounded spreading crown is fairly dense.

Leaves and bark. The smooth-margined simple leaves are 2.5–8 in. (6–20 cm) long and sometimes longer, on petioles 1–1.5 in. (2.5–4 cm) long. Petioles and midribs are stout, appearing especially so on the rusty-colored emerging leaves. Mature leaves are shiny yellow green above, lighter below with pinkish veins. The bark, smooth to slightly fissured, is light-colored with white patches and numerous small round lenticels.

The longest leaves were about 6 in. (15 cm).

Flowers. Male and female flowers occur on separate trees, but both occur in 1–1.5 in. (1.5–4 cm)-diameter rounded clusters on 1–2 in. (2.5–5 cm)-long green stems. Male flowers, with protruding stamens, are showier than the females. Individual flowers are 5-petaled, tubular, and fragrant. Flowering starts before leaves reappear.

Fruits are 10-angled, with 5 small longitudinal ridges near the apex. They are red, becoming black when mature, and sticky (like Velcro). They fall from the tree as clusters. Fruits mature in late spring and through the summer.

Flower and bud clusters photographed on St. John in February; inset shows close-up of the tiny (male) flowers (less than 0.1 in., 0.2 cm across).

Habitat. *Pisonia subcordata* occurs in the drier deciduous forests of the islands, often together with gumbo-limbo, Eugenias, fishpoison tree, and tan-tan. It prefers full sun and has high salt- and wind-tolerance.

Uses. Water mampoo is planted as an ornamental for its shade, the unusual appearance of its trunk(s), and its fast growth. Preference is given to the male tree to avoid the sticky litter produced by the females. The wood is soft, lightweight, and non-durable. It has been used to make fish net floats. No references to medicinal uses were found.

Mature fruit cluster on a twig in March; each fruit was slightly over 0.5 in. (1.3 cm) long.

Psidium guajava L.

guava, common guava, *guayaba, goyavier* (and many other local names)

Myrtaceae (myrtle family)

Spreading open-grown tree, about 21 ft. (6.4 m) tall and 7 in. (18 cm) in diameter at the ground line below the branching point. Photographed at Gallows Bay, St. Croix, in March.

This small tree is the source of the guava juice, jams, and many other food products of commerce. Guava is one of the most important tropical fruits worldwide. It is identified from its (1) opposite, simple leaves, aromatic when crushed, smooth-margined, with prominent sunken, parallel veins running from the midrib to the leaf edge; (2) usually multiple trunks arising from a single base near the ground, and having smooth, mottled bark; (3) flowers with 4–5 wide, separated petals, and with centers that look like delicate brushes due to the 200 or so protruding white stamens; and (4) spherical to pear-shaped fruits, 2–4 in. (5–10 cm) in diameter, green becoming light yellow when mature and having a strong, pleasant odor when ripe. Leaves, flowers, and fruit can be seen year-round, except in the driest years. In the V.I. and south Florida, guava is a common invader of disturbed sites. Thought to be native to southern Mexico and Central America, guava has been planted throughout the world's tropics, in most areas becoming naturalized.

Form. Guava can have a single trunk reaching 12 or even 18 in. (30, 46 cm) in diameter, and can become 33 ft. (10 m) tall. Open-grown guava often forms thickets with wide-spreading crowns.

Leaves and bark. Leaves, 2–5 in. (5–13 cm) long and 1–2 in. (2.5–5 cm) wide, are an attractive green above and paler below. The copper-colored bark flakes off to reveal patches of greenish underlayer.

Flowers are about 1.5 in. (4 cm) across. They occur along branches in leaf bases, on stems about 1 in. (2.5 cm) long. Petals do not last long, turning brown before falling.

Fruits are somewhat variable, but generally they are as described above. The pulp is yellow to red, even white in some cultivated varieties. Many hard angular seeds about 0.1 in. (2.5 mm) long are embedded in the fruit. These are dispersed widely by birds and other animals.

Habitat. *Psidium guajava* is tolerant of most soil types. It is drought-tolerant, somewhat tolerant of salt, and moderately wind-resistant. It prefers full sun, but can tolerate some shade.

Uses. Improved varieties of guava have been developed to have sweet, and in some varieties seedless, fruits. Guava products are widely exported to temperate parts of the world. The wood, strong and heavy, is valued for use in tool handles. The heartwood is brown or reddish-brown and the sapwood much paler. Various folk medicines and health products have been and are prepared from all parts of the tree. For example, extracts of roots, bark, and leaves are used to treat gastroenteritis, high blood pressure, vomiting, diarrhea, headache, and toothache, and the fruit juice to treat diarrhea, hepatitis, and gonorrhea. Tea made from the leaves is widely used to control blood sugar of diabetics in Japan and elsewhere.

Largest leaf was about 5 in. (13 cm) long, photographed in May on St. Croix.

Flowers, photographed in November on St. Croix, were about 1.5 in. (4 cm) across.

Mature fruit harvested in May on St. Croix. The largest one was about 3.5 in. (9 cm) in diameter.

Randia aculeata L.

box-briar, fishing-rod, Christmas-tree, white indigoberry, inkberry, *tintillo, petit coco*

Rubiaceae (madder family)

Multi-stemmed box-briar on the Lawaetz Museum grounds, St. Croix, in November. This specimen was about 20 ft. (6 m) tall.

In the V.I., box-briar serves as an unlikely Christmas tree. It has attractive green foliage and convenient thorns to hold ornaments. It is identified by its (1) gardenia-smelling white flowers, with petals that are 5-lobed, and have pale yellow centers; (2) small, nearly spherical fruits, green becoming white; (3) columnar shape, with long upright limbs beginning near the ground, each bearing rows of opposite twigs that end in paired gray thorns; and (4) simple, opposite, variably shaped but small leaves in clusters along twigs and near twig ends. Flowers and fruits are present nearly year-round. Native to the V.I. and south Florida, *R. aculeata* is found through the West Indies and into Venezuela. It is a rather common inhabitant of roadsides and agricultural savannas in drier areas.

Form. Box-briar is a small tree to 20 ft. (6 m) tall and 3 in. (7.6 cm) in trunk diameter.

Leaves and bark. Leaves vary in size and shape, 0.5–1.5 in. (1.3–4 cm) long and 0.25–1 in. (0.6–2.5 cm) across. The bark is gray to brown, smooth, becoming fissured and warty with age.

Flowers, about 0.6 in. (1.5 cm) across, have both male and female organs.

Fruits are 0.25–0.5 in. (0.6–1.3 cm) in diameter and stalkless. The purple to black pulp with several small rounded seeds is edible but not tasty.

Leaves and thorns on twigs, photographed in February on St. John; the longest were about 1.6 in. (4 cm). Inset shows mature fruit, 0.4 in. (1 cm) in diameter, photographed in February on St. Croix.

Habitat. Box-briar prefers full sun, and grows in rocky, uninviting soils as well as in agricultural soils. It is drought-, wind-, and salt-tolerant, so is found without much competition on some sites.

Uses. The long, slender, very strong branches, stripped of twigs and thorns, are used as fishing poles in the V.I. Box-briar is planted as a fragrant evergreen yard tree. Also, because it responds well to pruning, it is used to create formidable hedges. It is apparently not as commonly planted in south Florida. A dark blue dye can be made from the mature berries.

Flower, about 0.6 in. (1.6 cm) in diameter, in May on St. Croix.

The leaves, fruit, and sap have been used in folk medicines. For example, fruits are used in herbal medicine to control dysentery, fever, coughs, and colds, and the latex is reported to stop bleeding. The light brown wood is hard and heavy, but the trees are too small for the wood to be very useful.

Rhizophora mangle L.

red mangrove, mangrove, mangle, *mangle colorado, manglier rouge*

Rhizophoraceae (mangrove family)

Red mangrove thicket at Coral Bay, St. John, in March. Trees were approximately 40 ft. (12 m) high.

2 in.
5 cm

Red mangrove is usually the dominant component of the sea side of mangrove forests. This evergreen tree is identified by its (1) thick mass of branching, arching roots coming out from the lower trunk; (2) long, conspicuous pointed terminal buds on the twigs; (3) small yellow flowers with purple centers, (4) odd fruit that germinates on the tree, sending down a long-pointed primary root; and (5) tendency to form densely tangled thickets. Flowers and fruits are always present. The tree is native to southern Florida down through the Keys, the Bahamas, and through the West Indies except Dominica. Red mangrove is in fact found nearly throughout the world's tropics. It is very common in the V.I. and south Florida. Its range extends above the 29th parallel on both Florida coasts.

Form. Red mangrove trees can become almost 100 ft. (30 m) tall and 20 in. (51 cm) in trunk diameter, but are much smaller in the V.I. and south Florida, perhaps because of recurring hurricane damage. The many arching roots often obscure the base of the trunk. The crowns of mangrove thickets create a continuous cover.

Leaves. The somewhat leathery leaves are simple and opposite, 2.5–4 in. (6–10 cm) long and 1–2.5 in. (2.5–6.4 cm) wide, on petioles 0.5 in. (1.3 cm) or shorter.

Flowers occur in twos and fours on lateral forking stems, and have both male and female organs.

Fruits are green, becoming dark brown with maturity. The germinating fruits hang down on the tree until they fall from their increasing weight; they can become 12 in. (30 cm) long while on the tree. The fallen germinated fruit may float for over a year before lodging in a suitably protected site to grow. The fruit, including the protruding root, is edible.

Habitat. Found in protected seaside, silted, and muddy or sandy salt flats, red mangrove obviously is very salt-tolerant, and its masses of roots act as braces in the muck. The tree prefers full sun. Mangrove forests recover quickly from hurricanes.

Uses. Red mangrove is ecologically a crucially important tree worldwide, not only stabilizing shorelines, but also providing habitat and breeding grounds for countless species of sea creatures. The trees do well in hurricanes, and some owners lash their boats inside red mangrove forests to ride them out. The wood, hard and heavy, has many local uses, from charcoal to fence posts, and where trees get large enough, finds its way into lumber for cabinetry, boat construction, and many other products. Extracts of various parts of the tree have been used to treat angina, asthma, sore throat, hemorrhage, rheumatism, backache, diarrhea, dyspepsia, eye ailments, parasitic worm diseases, and even leprosy and cancer.

Twig end showing terminal bud and leaves, which were up to 6 in. (15 cm) long.

Flowers, photographed in south Florida, were nearly 1 in (2.5 cm) across.

Fruit shown here was about 5.5 in. (14 cm) long.

Leaves compound, pinnate

Compound pinnate leaves have a single petiole/midrib arising from the twig, and from which leaflets arise. There is a good bit of variation among compound pinnate leaves, as illustrated by the images here. It might be noted that compound pinnate leaves can be alternate or opposite on the twig. In this book, only *Guaiacum officinale* (lignum vitae) and *Tecoma stans* (ginger-thomas) have opposite pinnately compound leaves. Leaflets along the midrib of pinnately compound leaves are usually but not always paired opposite one another.

Guaiacum officinale (lignum vitae)

Tecoma stans (ginger-thomas)

Melicoccus bijugatus (genip)

Andira inermis (angelin)

Andira inermis (W. Wright) Kunth ex DC

angelin, bastard mahogany, cabbage angelin, *moca, bois olive*

Fabaceae (pea family)

Angelin in flower off Queen Mary highway, St. Croix, approximately 40 ft. (12 m) tall and 14 in. (36 cm) in trunk diameter below the fork. May.

Angelin is an attractive tree with a big crown of handsome leaves, and is especially noticeable when in full bloom, with large numbers of dark pink sweetpealike blossoms. It is identified by its: (1) alternate, pinnately compound leaves with odd numbers of leaflets; (2) showy flowers that have a sweet fragrance; and (3) distinctive fruits. A characteristic of angelin is the unpleasant rotting cabbage odor given off when the bark is cut. *Andira inermis* is native to the V.I., southern Mexico and south to Bolivia and Peru, and has been planted widely in other tropical areas. Angelin is common on the U.S.V.I. and Tortola, less so on Virgin Gorda; it is found but not common in south Florida.

Form. *Andira inermis* usually has a single trunk with a somewhat spreading and densely foliaged evergreen crown. It can grow to over 100 ft. (30 m) tall and to a diameter of 3 ft. (91 cm), though it is smaller in the V.I. and Florida.

Leaves and bark. Leaves are 6–16 in. (15–41 cm) long, with 7–13 leaflets, each 2–5 in. (5–13 cm) long and 1–2 in. (2.5–5 cm) broad. They have smooth margins. The bark is distinctive: light gray, fissured, and scaly.

Flowers are present much of the year, and are especially abundant in January and February and again from May to September. They occur in broad, branched, erect clusters, 6–12 in. (15–31 cm) long that are both terminal and lateral. Individual flowers are about 0.5 in. (1.3 cm) long.

Fruits are found all year. They are ovoid, single, about 1.5 in. (4 cm) long, slightly soft outside and hard within. They are borne offset on short stalks. The single seed is poisonous.

Habitat. Angelin is a hardy and adaptable tree. It does well even in the driest years. It tolerates some shade and is moderately salt-tolerant.

Uses. *Andira inermis* wood, where still available, is used to make attractively figured furniture. The wood's strength and the durability of the heartwood led to many uses in construction and other general applications in the past. The major use of this tree today is for its beauty and shade. Despite potent toxicity, the bark, roots and fruit have been used in folk medicines, for example against ringworm, intestinal worms, and to treat skin rash and wounds. Modern scientific studies have revealed antimalarial activity in identified components.

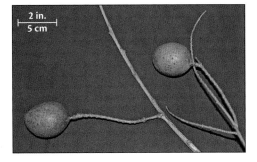

Note: Smoke from burning wood can cause serious eye damage, and wood dust has been reported to cause a dermatitis. Seeds, bark, and roots are poisonous.

Azadirachta indica A. Juss.

neem, *margosa, margosier du Vietnam*

Meliaceae (mahogany family)

Open-grown tree on the grounds of Caneel Bay resort, St. John, in February; approximate size: 33 ft. (10 m) tall and 14 in. (36 cm) in diameter below the branching point.

Neem is one of the most fascinating trees anywhere because of the many useful chemicals it makes. This evergreen tree is identified by its: (1) pinnately compound leaves with toothed-edge leaflets; (2) clustering of leaves at the ends of the upward-pointing, slender branches; (3) reddish bark and new leaves; (4) prominent elongated clusters of small white flowers; and (5) light yellow fruit in thin clusters. There aren't any full-grown trees in the V.I. or south Florida because of its recent introduction (about 35 years ago). Good specimens can be found at Caneel Bay on St. John. Native to India, neem has been planted widely in the world's tropics. It is common on Tortola, and found but not yet common on the other islands and south Florida. Neem has become naturalized, however, and is rapidly becoming more common.

Form. Neem is a graceful tree, usually with a single trunk. The crown is of medium density, often with individual branches protruding. The trees can attain heights of up to 100 ft. (30 m) in India, with trunk diameters up to 36 in. (91 cm).

Leaves and bark. Leaves are 12 in. (30 cm) or more in length, with 9–15 shiny leaflets. They are alternate, spiraling around the branches. The bark is gray with scaly plates and fissures exposing a reddish underlayer.

2 in.
5 cm

Images made in March on St. John.

Flowers, appearing in the spring, are small (about 0.4 in. [1 cm] across), and occur in branched clusters 2–6 in. (5–15 cm) long. They are white, and have a sweet, jasminelike fragrance.

Fruits resemble olives, 0.5–0.75 in. (1.3–1.9 cm) long, with a single elliptical stone. They occur in clusters like the flowers. Bitter at first, they attain a pleasant taste when mature, and are relished in some locales.

Habitat. *Azadirachta indica* is a hardy tree. It survives drought and high winds, and stony, shallow, and acidic soils (as long as the soil is well drained). It is also salt-tolerant, so it survives in areas where few other trees can. However, it is killed if its roots are inundated more than for brief periods of time. The tree prefers full sunlight.

Uses. Because of neem's many uses, the U.S. Department of Agriculture began studying it in 1972. The National Academy of Sciences later (1992) published a study, "Neem: A Tree for Solving Global Problems." The report stimulated even more research, and much is now known. The tree produces many complex chemicals with useful properties. A search of the Web reveals a large number of commercially available neem products—from lotions to insecticides. The most studied chemical is azadirachtin, which is a potent insecticide with activity against many pests, and

Image made in the V.I. in May.

with no known toxicity to humans or other warm-blooded animals, or to plants. This and other chemicals are found in highest concentration in the seeds. Preparations from neem parts have many medicinal uses, particularly in India. Neem is being cultivated as a source of chemicals, many of which have molecular structures too complicated to be made commercially in the laboratory. Neem was originally introduced into the V.I. as a shade tree, and is still planted for that purpose. Unfortunately, neem is invasive in the V.I. and is rapidly becoming a problem in some areas. The tree is also grown elsewhere for its fruit, to help retard desertification in some areas of the world (sub-Saharan Africa), and for its wood. The latter is hard and heavy, easy to season, and resistant to termites and decay. The sapwood is light-colored and the heartwood is red to red-brown, like mahogony. It finds use in general construction, furniture-making, paneling, posts, poles and other products. Because the tree grows rapidly, it is used for firewood production in some areas.

Bursera simaruba (L.) Sarg.

gumbo-limbo, turpentine tree, *almácigo, gommier rouge*

Burseraceae (bursera family)

Well-formed tree 45 ft. (14 m) tall and 31 in. (78 cm) in dbh, on the campus of the University of the Virgin Islands in May.

Bursera simaruba is in the same large family as frankincense and myrrh (which are obtained from the resin of small trees native to the Arabian Peninsula). Amusingly, gumbo-limbo is also known as "tourist tree" because of its reddish bark that peels off like sunburned skin. It is easily recognized by its (1) red-brown, peeling bark with underlying green patches; (2) pinnately compound leaves with reddish petioles and midribs; (3) turpentine odor of crushed leaves and resin; and (4) when present, flowers and fruit. Gumbo-limbo is native to the West Indies, including the V.I., and to south Florida. It is common.

Form. Usually gumbo-limbo has a single trunk, which can be up to 36 in. (91 cm) in diameter. Trees can attain a height of 80 ft. (24 m), but are usually shorter in the V.I. and south Florida. They have large spreading branches and crowns of medium density.

Leaves. The alternate leaves are 4–8 in. (10–20 cm) long, with 3–7 smooth-edged leaflets, each 1.25–3 in. (3.2–7.6 cm) long and 0.75–1.5 in. (2–4 cm) across. Gumbo-limbo is briefly deciduous, leaves falling during January and February. The leaves grow back quickly. The bark is relatively smooth, except for the thin peeling sheets.

Photographed in May.

Flowers are small, white, and occur in narrow terminal clusters that are 2–6 in. (5–15 cm) long. Each flower is 5-lobed and about 0.2 in. (0.5 cm) across. Gumbo-limbo blooms in the spring about the same time as new leaves appear. Both male and female flowers usually occur on different trees, although some flowers are bisexual.

Fruits. Resembling small 3-sided olives, the fruits are about 0.25 in. (0.6 cm) wide and 0.5 (1.3 cm) long, borne on stalks of the same length. They appear shortly after the flowers in late spring or early summer. They are green when young and mature to an attractive red color. Birds eat the ripe fruits and spread the seeds. When fully mature, fruits split into three parts, revealing a three-angled whitish seed.

Habitat. *Bursera simaruba* is very drought-resistant, salt-tolerant, and wind-resistant, and is found close to the sea as well as in the hills. It is native to limestone-derived soils.

Flower clusters on a tree in Key West, Florida, in April; inset shows close-up of flowers.

Uses. Gumbo-limbo is used as a landscape ornamental in the V.I. and south Florida. The wood, although weak, is used in interior construction, crating, boxes, and plywood; but its light weight and susceptibility to blue stain, decay, and invasion by insects limit its use. Commercial wood products usually come from Mexico. Severed larger branches, which root readily, have been used as living fence posts. The resin and extracts of other plant parts have been used in folk medicines to treat, among other problems, wounds, gout, toothache, fever, kidney stones, snakebite, gangrene, and lung infections. The resin has also been used for incense, as well as insect repellent, glue, and varnish. The leaves have been used to make a tea substitute, and as fodder.

Cassia fistula L.

golden-shower, shower-of-gold, *cañafístula, caneficier*

Fabaceae (pea family)

This tree, with immature fruit, was photographed in March on the grounds of the Caneel Bay resort, St. John; it was about 20 ft. (6 m) tall and 6 in. (15 cm) in dbh.

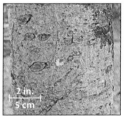

When in bloom, this is one of the prettiest trees in the V.I. and south Florida. Native to India, golden-shower has been planted throughout the tropics for its beautiful golden-yellow blossoms. The tree is identified by its (1) flowers (spring and summer); (2) big, persistent seed pods with a licorice-smelling pulp; and (3) large pinnately compound leaves. It apparently has not escaped from cultivation in the V.I. or south Florida, and is not especially common. Handsome specimens can be seen on the grounds of Caneel Bay resort on St. John and in Fairchild Tropical Botanic Garden in Coral Gables, Florida.

Form. Usually short-trunked, with a wide-spreading open crown, *C. fistula* can attain heights and breadths of 50 ft. (15 m) or more and trunk diameters of 18 in. (46 cm). In the V.I. and south Florida the tree is usually much smaller.

Leaves and bark. The alternate leaves are 12–16 in. (30–41 cm) long. The 8–16 leaflets are thin, short-stalked, and 3–6 in. (7.5–15 cm) long and 1.75–2.75 in. (4.4–7 cm) across. They are usually bright green, but become dark and dull with age. In the V.I., old leaves fall throughout the year, and new ones emerge, so the tree, although technically not evergreen, is rarely devoid of green leaves. In south Florida, the trees lose their leaves briefly in winter. The bark is smooth and gray, becoming rougher with age.

Leaf, photographed in March.

Flowers occur in drooping clusters 8–24 in. (20–61 cm) long. Each delicate flower, about 2 in. (5 cm) across, has five bright yellow petals about 1 in. (2.5 cm) long and elliptic. Ten stamens are of two lengths: three are very long and seven much shorter.

Fruits. Pods are green, becoming dark purple-brown when mature (about 1 year). They are round, 15–24 in. (38–61 cm) long and about 0.75 in. (1 cm) in diameter. Pods have many cross walls which create compartments, each of which contains a single orange-brown seed surrounded by a sweet, sticky pulp. The pulp attracts birds and other animals, which eat it and disperse the seeds.

Flower cluster in May, about 13 in. (33 cm) long, in crown.

Habitat. Golden-shower tolerates a diversity of soils, but does best on fertile well-drained sites. It prefers full sun, and is salt- and drought-tolerant.

Uses. *Cassia fistula* is mainly grown as an ornamental in the V.I. However, the tree has a very rich history of medicinal uses, especially in India. Decoctions of various plant parts have been (and perhaps still are) used in the West Indies to treat skin diseases, fever, worms, gout, and rheumatism, and as a diuretic. The fruit pulp is strongly purgative; indeed, the tree is known as "purging cassia" in some places. The wood is reddish, hard, heavy, strong, and durable. It has been used in construction, cabinetry, as fence posts, and to make farm implements.

Golden shower is a prolific producer of fruit; here the pods, photographed in March, averaged about 12 in. (30 cm) in length. Inset shows an open, mature fruit with seeds imbedded in the pulp; this pod had a diameter of about 0.75 in. (2 cm).

Cedrela odorata L.

Spanish-cedar, *cedro hembra, acajou rouge*

Meliaceae (mahagony family)

Fairly large Spanish-cedar at La Reine, St. Croix, in February; tree was about 70 ft. (21 m) tall and 33 in. (84 cm) in dbh.

Spanish-cedar is the most important timber species in tropical America. It is imported into the southern U.S. for use in cabinetry. It is identified by its (1) large, pinnately compound leaves; (2) the garlic odor of crushed leaves, twigs, and flowers; (3) the woody seed capsules, which split open into five sections and remain on the tree for much of the year; and (4) characteristic bark with large vertical fissures. The tree is not a cedar; rather its name reflects the appearance and aroma of its wood, reminiscent of cedars. It is native to the V.I., other West Indian islands, and parts of Central and South America, and has been planted widely elsewhere, including south Florida. For several reasons, it has resisted plantation cultivation, but its value is assuring continued research. The species is found but is not common on St. Croix, is rare on the other U.S.V.I, and is not found in the B.V.I.

Form. Under favorable conditions, *C. odorata* grows rapidly into a tall (to 100 ft., 30 m) tree with a large, rounded crown and trunk diameter of 36 in. (91 cm) or more. It is an attractive tree, planted for shade. Large trees sometimes have buttressed bases.

Leaves and bark. The leaves are alternate, with even numbers of 10–22 leaflets. Leaves are long—1–2 ft. (0.3–0.6 m) overall—and leaflets, drooping on slender stalks, are 2–6 in. (5–15 cm) long. Their edges are smooth. The trees lose their leaves in the dry season (Dec.–Jan.), with new leaves appearing with the rains. The thick bark is gray to brown.

Flowers, which appear June to August, are narrow, yellow-green, and tube-shaped, only about 0.4 in. (1 cm) long. They occur in long (6–16 in., 15–41 cm), loosely branched terminal clusters.

Fruits are green, becoming brown with maturity. They are elliptical seed capsules, and occur in terminal branched clusters. When fully mature they split open, releasing 40–50 winged seeds about 0.75 in. (2 cm) long.

Habitat. Fairly tolerant of soil type as long as it is well drained, Spanish-cedar needs a dry season and full sun. It is drought-tolerant, moderately salt-tolerant, and fairly wind-resistant.

Uses. The narrow sapwood of *C. odorata* is light brown, and the heartwood pinkish to reddish-brown. It is unusual among tropical woods in having growth rings. It darkens somewhat with age and exposure to light. It is soft but strong, easy to work, and resistant to decay and termites. These properties and its pleasant odor are responsible for its wide variety of uses, from cigar boxes (in Cuba) and clothes chests to window frames and furniture. The hollowed-out trunks were once used to make dugout canoes. The bitter inner bark has been used in folk medicines for treatments of epilepsy, psoriasis, and malaria, and probably other maladies. Spanish-cedar is a good source of nectar for honey bees.

The overall length of this leaf, photographed in February, was 12 in. (30 cm).

Cluster of flowers in crown; inset shows close-up of flowers. Photographs were made by Jozef Keularts in May on St. Croix.

Cluster of mature fruit, in February, ready to split open; the largest fruits were about 1.2 in. (3 cm) long. Inset shows open fruits and a seed; the seed was 0.75 in. (2 cm) long.

Gliricidia sepium (Jacq.) Kunth. ex Walp.

pea-tree, gliricidia, mother-of-cocoa, quick-stick, *mata-ratón, gliceridia*

Fabaceae (pea family)

Typical disheveled-looking pea-tree on the campus of the University of the Virgin Islands, St. Thomas, in February. This tree was about 30 ft. (9 m) tall and over 12 in. (30 cm) in trunk diameter near the ground.

Native from Mexico south through Central America and northern South America, pea-tree has been planted in most of the world's tropics. It is fairly common on many West Indian islands. The tree is identified from its (1) pinnately compound leaves; (2) beautiful pea blossomlike flowers; (3) flat, light greenish-yellow pods, which become black as they mature from summer to winter; and (4) the rather open, gangly appearance of the crown. Flowers and/or fruit are usually present. The tree is found but not especially common in south Florida, and on all the V.I., being perhaps most common on Tortola. It has escaped cultivation, so will probably become more common.

Form. *Gliricidia sepium* is a small tree to 33 ft (10 m) tall and 10 in. (25 cm) or more in trunk diameter. Its crown is made up of a tangled mass of limbs, but its foliage is sparce, giving the crown a thin appearance. The tree frequently has multiple trunks originating near the ground. Pea-tree loses its leaves in the dry season.

Leaves are most commonly alternate, 6–16 in. (15–41 cm) long overall, with 7–17 leaflets, each 1.25–2.5 in. (3–6 cm) long and 0.5–1.25 in. (1.3–3 cm) wide.

Flowers are borne in clusters on the leafless branches in the dry season.

Fruits are pods 4–6 in. (10–15 cm) long and about 0.5 in. (1.3 cm) wide. Each contains 3–8 nearly round flat brown seeds.

Habitat. Pea-tree tolerates a range of soil types, is high in drought tolerance, and moderately resistant to salt. It therefore grows in a variety of habitats. Because of its small size and open crown, it probably is wind-resistant.

Uses. The pan-tropical planting of the very fast-growing *Gliricidia sepium* has been for coffee and cocoa shade, living fences, forage, and biomass fuel. It is also used as an ornamental. The tree is easily propagated from cuttings—even fence post–size ones—and quickly regenerates when branches are cut off for forage. Roots harbor nitrogen-fixing bacteria. Interestingly, the leaves and other plant parts are toxic to non-ruminant animals, and in fact extracts are used as a rodenticide. The word gliricidia means "rodent killer" in Latin. Many uses in folk medicine include treatment of hair loss, boils, bruises, colds, wounds, cough, headache, and even tumors, gonorrhea, gangrene, and rheumatism. Modern chemical analyses of extracts have identified a plethora of chemicals, some with medicinal potential. The sapwood of pea-tree is light brown and the heartwood dark brown, turning dark reddish-brown. It is resistant to decay and insects, making it useful for outdoor construction

The largest leaves here were about 10 in. (25 cm) long.

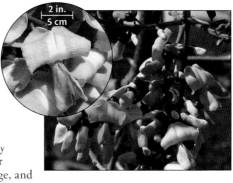

Nearly mature fruit pod in tree, about 6 in. (15 cm) long.

Guaiacum officinale L.

lignum vitae, *guayacán, gaïac*

Zygophyllaceae (caltrop family)

Handsome lignum vitae tree at Caneel Bay resort, St. John. The specimen was about 25 ft. (7.6 m) tall and 12 in. (30 cm) in trunk diameter just below its branching point.

Lignum vitae is noted for having the heaviest wood in the world. Its wood also is among the most durable; in the V.I., an intact fencepost used by Taina Indians was found by radiocarbon dating to be 800 years old. Lignum vitae is an evergreen, identified by its (1) blue 4-petaled flowers; (2) distinctive odd-shaped fruits; (3) opposite, pinnately compound leaves with 4–6 stalkless leaflets, an unusual kind of leaf; and (4) distinctive mottled bark. Native to the West Indies, and once plentiful in the V.I., the original trees were cut for their very valuable wood. The species is fairly common on St. Croix and St. John, and is found on the other Virgin Islands. Several fine specimens are on the grounds of the Whim Museum and Lawaetz Plantation on St. Croix, and on the Caneel Bay resort grounds on St. John. This species has been planted in south Florida, but a related species, *Guaiacum sanctum* (also called lignum vitae, native to Florida), is more common. It is distinguished from *G. officinale* by usually having more (6–10) leaflets per leaf, and shorter leaflets.

Form. *Guaiacum officinale* can grow to 30 ft. (9 m) in height, and can have trunk diameters of 18 in. (46 cm), occasionally more. Trees frequently have distorted trunks and branches. Twigs have many wide-angled forks. Crowns are well proportioned, rounded, and very dense.

Leaves and bark. Leaves are 1.5–3 in. (4–7.6 cm) long, with leaflets being 0.75–2 in. (2–5 cm) long and 0.5–1.25 in. (1.3–3 cm) across. The smallest leaflets are at the base. The bark is light brown, with plates flaking off, leaving both lighter patches and dark gray-green areas.

Flowers. The blue flowers are a rarity for trees in the West Indies and south Florida. Dark at first, they fade, so a single tree will have various shades of blue flowers. They are usually about 1 in. (2.5 cm) across (or larger) with stems about 0.75 in. (2 cm) long. Flowers are seen after rains from early spring to fall.

Fruits are green at first, turning orange-brown when mature. They are flattened 2-chambered capsules, heart-shaped and about 0.75 in. (2 cm) in diameter. They are on stalks about 0.75 in. (2 cm) long. Each fruit splits open along four seams to reveal two red fleshy seed coverings. Seeds are elongated and about 0.5 in. (1.3 cm) in diameter.

Habitat. Lignum vitae is very drought- wind- and salt-tolerant, once being most abundant in dry coastal areas. It grows optimally in limestone-derived, well-drained soils. It prefers full sun.

Uses. The wood of *G. officinale* is tough, strong, and very hard. The narrow sapwood is pale yellow and the heartwood is dark greenish-brown to nearly black. The heartwood is self-lubricating due to its wax and oil content, making it very valuable in the past for bearings, bushing blocks, pulleys, etc. in sailing and steam ships. Today it is more of a novelty, used in carvings. An extract of the wood was long used in official medicine as a stimulant and to increase perspiration, and before that the resin and wood extracts were used against a variety of maladies, including venereal diseases, gout, rheumatism, skin diseases, and fever.

These flowers were about 1.25 in. (3 cm) across.

Mature fruit in crown, some open, revealing the bright red seed coat. Inset shows mature fruit before opening.

Haematoxylum campechianum L.

logwood, bloodwoodtree, *campeche, bois campêche*

Fabaceae (pea family)

Small tree at St. George Village Botanical Garden, St. Croix; this tree measured about 15 ft. (4.6 m) in height and 6 in. (15 cm) in trunk diameter at the base. Inset shows bark of a much larger tree also at SGVBG.

3 in.
7.5 cm

A purple dye extracted from the heartwood of logwood once made this an important commercial tree. In fact, the dye is still used as the biological tissue stain haematoxylin. Synthetic dyes have replaced it for other uses. This small nearly evergreen tree is identified by its (1) clusters of papery, light brown, leaflike pods (which persist and are usually present); (2) showy, pale yellow, pendant clusters of very fragrant flowers (Dec.–May); (3) shaggy, tortuously fluted trunk—or usually multiple trunks; (4) dark green, pinnately compound leaves with heart-shaped leaflets; and (5) sharp spines that lurk in its foliage. It is a native to the Yucatan Peninsula, Guatemala, and Belize, and has been widely planted in the West Indies, where it has become naturalized. Although the tree is fairly common on St. Croix, it is rare—if found at all—on St. Thomas, and is apparently absent on the other islands. It has been planted in south Florida.

Form. *Haematoxylum campechianum* reaches 40 ft. (12 m) in height and a trunk diameter of 20 in. (51 cm) or more. It usually branches near the ground. The crown is bulky, heavy-limbed, and unkempt-looking, often broader than the tree is tall.

Leaves and bark. Leaves are alternate, with even numbers of leaflets (4–8 pairs per leaf). Leaves are 2–4 in. (5–10 cm) long and leaflets 0.5–1.5 in. (1.3–4 cm) long and almost as broad. Spines are found at the bases of many leaves. The bark is light brown or gray, smooth, becoming furrowed, and frequently peeling off in strings as the tree ages.

Flowers are in elongated clusters 1–3 in. (2.5–7.6 cm) long and about 1 in. (2.5 cm) in diameter. Individual flowers are about 0.5 in. (1.3 cm) broad and long, including their stalks. Each has 5 petals and 10 protruding stamens.

Flower clusters (Feb., St. Croix) are showy en masse; inset shows a bud cluster and thorn.

Fruits. Seed pods are 1–2.5 in. (2.5–6.4 cm) long and about 0.5 in. (1.3 cm) wide, borne in bundles. In an unusual fashion for legumes, they split open down the middle instead of along the edges. Each contains 1–3 oblong flat seeds about 0.4 in. (1 cm) long.

Habitat. Logwood is an invader of dry areas, but can tolerate and thrive in areas that have extended inundation. It is also tolerant of salt, drought, wind, and various soil types. It prefers full sun.

Uses. Besides being a source of dye, the wood, which is very durable, has been used as fence posts and in cabinetwork. When first sawed, it is orange and has the odor of violets, but becomes dark red and odorless on exposure to air. It is very hard and heavy. Logwood is planted as an ornamental because of its showy flowers—and because it can form an excellent barrier when desired. Bees are attracted to the flowers. Extracts of the wood have been used in folk medicine to treat nerve disorders, hepatitis, anemia, headache, dysentery, and diarrhea, and as an antibiotic. Bacteria associated with the roots fix nitrogen, enriching the soil.

Melicoccus bijugatus Jacq.

genip, genep, kinep, Spanish lime, *mamoncillo, quenepa, knepe*

Sapindaceae (soapberry family)

Open-grown tree on the grounds of the Caneel Bay resort, St. John. The tree was about 50 ft. (15 m) tall and had a dbh of 18 in. (46 cm). Thinning in the upper crown might have reflected the time of year (early March).

You can buy the flavorful, green, grapelike fruits of genip along the roadside in the V.I. and parts of south Florida from June to September. The evergreen tree is recognized by its (1) erect form with dense symmetrical crown; (2) branches that are red when young; and (3) pinnately compound leaves with four paired leaflets. The leaf's central midrib frequently has prominent wings. Native to Columbia, Venezuela, and bordering areas, it has been widely planted in the West Indies, south Florida, and other tropical areas. It is common on the major Virgin Islands and in south Florida. A related species, *Sapindus saponaria* (soapberry), is common in south Florida and found but not common in the V.I.

Form. Usually a single stout trunk supports a nicely rounded crown. This attractive tree can attain a height of 85 ft. (26 m) and trunk diameter of 36 in. (91 cm) but is usually smaller in the V.I. and south Florida. The trunk is sometimes fluted. Branches are numerous and tend to point upward.

Leaves and bark. Leaves are alternate, 6–8 in. (15–20 cm) long overall, with the central axis being about 3 in. (7.5 cm) long, and the terminal pair of leaflets being larger than the other two. They are light green. The bark has irregular warty projections from its otherwise smooth surface.

Leaves and flower cluster.

Close-up of flowers.

Flowers are in terminal, cylindrical clusters 3–6 in. (7.6–15 cm) long, on narrow stalks off a central stem. Individual flowers are greenish-white, about 0.2 in. (0.5 cm) across, with male flowers having protruding stamens. Flowering is from April to June. Some trees have both male and female flowers, and some have only one sex. The flowers are fragrant and attractive to bees.

Fruits are borne in grapelike clusters. Individual fruits have a tough leathery skin and are about 1 in. (2.5 cm) in diameter. They have an edible but thin yellow-orange pulp when ripe, with one and sometimes two large round seeds.

Habitat. Genip is a robust tree that prefers full sun and well-drained soils. Its high tolerance to salt, wind, and drought makes it at home in most parts of the V.I. and south Florida.

Leaf detail. The longest leaflets were about 6 in. (15 cm). Photos were taken in May on St. John.

Uses. *Melicoccus bijugatus* is planted widely as a shade and fruit tree. Because it is hardy, it will grow where most other trees will not. Jams and jellies are sometimes made from the ripe fruit. The wood, light brown to pale yellow-brown, hard and of medium density, is used locally in construction, cabinetry, etc., even though it is not durable. A decoction of the leaves and stems has been used to treat coughs, nerve disorders, and fever, and extracts of the seeds to treat diarrhea.

Clusters of nearly ripe fruit in May on St. Croix.

Piscidia carthagenensis Jacq.

fishpoison tree, dogwood, *ventura, bois à enivrer*

Fabaceae (pea family)

Typical tree with fruit at St. George Village Botanical Garden, St. Croix, in May; this specimen was about 22 ft. (6.7 m) tall and 10 in. (25 cm) in diameter. Inset shows bark of another tree at SGVBG.

Roots, young leaves, and inner bark of this tree contain a chemical that temporarily stuns fish. Carib Indians threw these tree parts into ponds, and stunned fish floated to the surface for easy harvesting. Fishpoison tree is identified by its (1) prominently veined, pinnately compound leaves; (2) large colorful clusters of flowers when present (Feb.–June); and (3) distinctive fruit in clusters, appearing in the summer and persisting for several months. *Piscidia carthagenensis* is native to the V.I. and most other West Indian islands, as well as the coasts of east and west central America and into Venezuela. It is common on the major Virgin Islands, just how common being readily seen when the trees have their large fruit clusters. This species does not occur in south Florida, although a very closely related and very similar one does: *Piscidia piscipula,* "Florida fishpoison tree"; it is very common.

Form. *Piscidia carthagenensis* is a small to medium-size tree, usually with its trunk branching near the ground. It can attain heights of 40–50 ft. (12–15 m) and trunk diameters to 24 in. (61 cm). The crown is frequently sparse, irregularly rounded, and often unkempt-looking.

Leaves and bark. The leaves are alternate, 7–12 in. (18–30 cm) long, with 5–11 relatively large leaflets 3–7 in. (7.6–18 cm) long and up to 4 in. (10 cm) broad. They are green above and gray-green below. Trees are leafless in late winter and early spring for a few weeks. The bark is gray, fissured on older trees, with scattered whitish patches or scales.

Flowers occur in 3–10 in. (7.6–25 cm)-long branched clusters, usually upright and lateral on twigs. Individual flowers resemble those of sweet pea, with pinkish-white petals arising from a darker base, about 0.6 in. (1.6 cm) long, on delicate stems.

Flower and bud cluster in March on St. Croix; buds were about 0.4 in. (1 cm) long.

Fruits are unusual pods with four longitudinal papery vanes, light yellow-green becoming light brown when mature, and occurring in tight clusters. Each pod contains several flat brown seeds about 0.25 in. (0.6 cm) long. Pods do not open, and eventually are wind-dispersed.

Habitat. Fishpoison tree has excellent drought- and salt-tolerance and moderate wind resistance, so it survives in habitats unfavorable for many other trees, and frequently is found on stony soils. It tolerates moderate shade but prefers full sun.

Uses. The wood is hard and heavy, attractive and durable. It is used locally for boat building, posts, furniture, and as firewood. Trees are planted as ornamentals for their showy flowers and unusual pods; the flowers attract bees and hummingbirds. In addition to its use to stun fish, fishpoison tree decoctions have reportedly been

Clusters of the odd fruit pods, photographed in May on St. Croix. Inset shows a single fruit and a seed.

used as folk remedies, including treatment of fungal infections of the skin. Extracts of various parts of *Piscidia piscipula* have been used for backache, toothache, headache, and ulcers, among several other maladies, obviously being used below toxic concentrations. The active ingredient in *P. piscipula* (and presumably *P. carthagensis*) responsible for stunning fish is rotenone, which has long been used commercially not only in fish control, but also as an insecticide.

Note: Extracts of tree parts are poisonous.

Spathodea campanulata P. Beauv.

African tuliptree, fountain-tree, *tulipán africano, tulipier du Gabon*

Bignoniaceae (catalpa family)

This tree, at the St. George Village Botanical Garden, St. Croix, was about 40 ft. (12 m) tall and 20 in. (51 cm) in diameter at the base.

African tuliptree, when in full bloom, is one of the world's showiest flowering trees. The tree is evergreen in the V.I. but loses its leaves in the winter in south Florida. It is easily identified by its (1) unusual brilliant red flowers, present all year (some varieties have yellow flowers); (2) large, persisting, upright, boat-shaped pods; and (3) long, dark green, opposite, pinnately compound leaves. Native to the moist African tropics, *S. campanulata* has been planted widely in the world's tropics as an ornamental. This is the only species in the genus *Spathodea*. It is common on St. Croix, where it has escaped cultivation, and is found but not especially common on the other major islands. It is fairly common in south Florida.

Form. On the best sites, *Spathodea campanulata* is a big tree, attaining heights of nearly 100 ft. (30 m) and trunk diameters of over 36 in. (91 cm). The rounded, dense, and irregularly shaped crown may be 40 ft. (12 m) or more wide. It usually has a single trunk with tall narrow buttresses and long drooping branches.

Leaves and bark. Leaves are 12–24 in. (30–61 cm) long overall. The 11–17 leaflets are leathery, 3–6 in. (7.5–15 cm) long, on short stalks. The bark is light brown, relatively smooth but becoming fissured with age.

Flowers are borne terminally in upright clusters which are about 4 in. (10 cm) high and 8 in. (20 cm) across. Numerous horn-shaped flower buds, 1–2 in. (2.5–5 cm) long, curve inward toward the cluster's center. These buds are filled with nectar, which can be squeezed out in a stream, behaving like a water pistol. They open a few at a time, last two days, and fall.

Common red flower clusters, with inset showing the yellow variety. Individual flowers were 4–5 in. (10–13 cm) across. Photos taken in May and February, respectively, on St. Croix.

Fruits are green, becoming dark brown, 5–10 in. (13–25 cm) long and about 1.5 in. (4 cm) wide, on short, stout stalks. Each pod contains 500 or so very thin, pointed seeds with transparent wings 0.5–1 in. (1.3–2.5 cm) across. The pods split open on one side to release the seeds, which are dispersed by the wind.

Habitat. African tuliptree grows in a variety of soils, but does best in deep, well-drained, moist soils on protected sites. It can tolerate some drought, but may lose most of its leaves. It is not wind-tolerant, prefers full sun, and is moderately salt-tolerant.

These nearly mature pods in March on St. Croix were about 9 in. (23 cm) long. Inset shows mature pod cut open to reveal winged seeds.

Uses. *Spathodea campanulata* is planted for its flowers and for the deep shade it creates. It is best to give it plenty of space: its roots can push up sidewalks, its brittle branches can break in the wind, and its trunk can become hollowed out by decay and insects, making the whole tree vulnerable to toppling over. The wood is soft, light, and brittle and is not used. Extracts of the bark, leaves, and flowers are used in folk medicine in Africa for treatment of gonorrhea, diarrhea, ulcers, fever, and as an aid in burn-healing.

Note: The seeds of this tree are poisonous.

Spondias mombin L.

yellow mombin, hogplum, *jobo, mombin, fruits jaunes*

Anacardiaceae (cashew family)

Yellow mombin tree in May at St. George Village Botanical Garden, St. Croix, approximately 52 ft. (16 m) tall and 20 in. (51 cm) in dbh.

Although in a family with many toxic members, yellow mombin has no poisonous properties. It is identified by its (1) numerous spiny or knoblike projections from its corky bark; (2) pinnately compound leaves; (3) masses of clusters of tiny fragrant flowers; (4) clusters of juicy fruits, green becoming yellow and fragrant with maturity; and (5) resin exuding from cuts in the bark. *Spondias mombin* is probably native to the V.I., other West Indies islands, tropical Mexico and south to Peru and northern Brazil. It has been introduced into south Florida.

Form. Yellow mombin is fast-growing, attaining heights of 65 ft. (20 m) or more and trunk diameters of 30 in. (76 cm) or more. It usually has a single trunk and an erect bearing.

Leaves are alternate, 8–16 in. (20–41 cm) long overall, with 9–19 thin leaflets, each 2–4 in. (5–10 cm) long and 1–1.75 in. (2.5–4.4 cm) broad.

Flower clusters are terminal, 6–12 in. (15–30 cm) long. Individual flowers are about 0.25 in. (0.6 cm) across, with male, female, and bisexual flowers on the same tree. The petals are white and the center stamens (males and bisexuals) tipped with yellow.

Fruits are about 1.5 in. (4 cm) long and 1 in. (2.5 cm) in diameter. They have a thin yellow flesh with a sour but pleasing taste surrounding a large stone holding 4–5 small seeds.

Habitat. *Spondias mombin* prefers full sun, but can tolerate some shade. It is tolerant of various types of soils and rainfall patterns. Trees may be found in dry areas but do best in moist habitats. Salt-tolerance and wind-resistance apparently are low.

Uses. Ripe fruits are consumed raw or made into jams and jellies. The juice is consumed raw (after sweetening), and also fermented into wine- and ciderlike drinks. The fruit is also a valued feed for cattle and pigs. The resin of yellow mombin is used as glue. The wood is yellow or yellow-brown with darker markings, lightweight but strong. Although not durable, it is widely used in carpentry, and to make a variety of products, from doctors' tongue depressors to packing crates. Extracts of the astringent bark serve as folk remedies for diarrhea, dysentery, hemorrhoids, and gonorrhea. Tea made from the flowers and leaves has been used to relieve stomachache, cystitis, malarial fever, and eye and throat inflammations. The gum reportedly expels tapeworms. Modern studies have identified many exotic chemicals in various tree parts.

Leaves on a branch in November, St. Croix.

Flower cluster in May on St. Croix; inset shows male or bisexual flowers close-up.

Nearly mature and mature fruit in crown, photographed on St. Croix by Jozef Keularts in August.

Swietenia macrophylla King

Honduras mahogany, *Caoba hondureña, acajou du Honduras*

Swietenia mahagoni Jacq.

West Indies mahogany, *caoba dominicana, acajou petites feuilles*

Meliaceae (mahogany family)

Open-grown mahogany in central St. Croix in May. This tree was
approximately 60 ft. (18 m) tall and 40 in. (102 cm) in dbh.

These true mahoganies produce one of the world's most desirable cabinet woods;
Chippendale furniture was made from them. Both species have been planted in
the V.I., where they have hybridized—especially on St. Croix—making it difficult
to sort out the two species. Only *S. mahagoni* occurs in south Florida. They are
identified by their (1) handsome form; (2) pinnately compound alternate leaves
with even numbers of smooth-margined leaflets; and especially (3) peculiar
upright fruit, which is present essentially all year. Where they haven't hybridized,
S. macrophylla is larger in leaf size, height, and especially fruit size. *Swietenia
macrophylla* is native from southern Mexico to the northern Amazon region,
whereas *S. mahagoni* is native from south Florida through the Keys, the Bahamas,
and through Hispaniola. Where moisture is sufficient (no prolonged dry period),
both are evergreens. They are common on all the V.I., although less so on Virgin
Gorda. Many fine specimens line the Queen Mary Highway on St. Croix.

Form. The mahoganies have clear erect trunks supporting rounded crowns of medium density. They reach heights of 60 ft. (18 m) or more and trunk diameters of 36 in. (91 cm) or more. Trunk bases may become somewhat buttressed with age.

Leaves and bark. Leaves of the two species vary from 4 to 16 in. (10–41 cm) in length, and have 4–12 leaflets. Leaflets are 1–6 in. (2.5-15 cm) long. The leaves of *S. mahagoni* are at the small end of the ranges, and those of hybrids in the middle. The scaly bark of the mahoganies is dark brown or gray.

This leaf, photographed on St. Croix, is probably from *S. mahagoni* or a hybrid.

Flowers occur in branched clusters arising from leaf bases on a single stem. Clusters are 2–6 in. (5–15 cm) long in both species. Individual flowers are 0.25–0.5 in. (0.6–1.3 cm) across and greenish-yellow. Male and female flowers are separate within the same cluster, and are very similar. Flowering is from spring to early summer in both species.

Flower clusters on a twig and detail, in May on St. John. Each flower was about 0.3 in. (0.7 cm) across.

Fruits are erect and egg-shaped, 2.5–7 in. (6–18 cm) long, with those of *S. mahagoni* occupying the small end of the range. They are borne on long, stout stalks. They take up to a year to mature, so trees almost always have fruits. When mature and after turning from green to dark brown, they split open along 5 seams from the base, releasing 350–450 winged seeds per fruit.

Habitat. The mahoganies grow in partial shade or full sun. Wind-, drought-, and salt-tolerant, they also tolerate a variety of soils from clays and rocky, alkaline ones to sand. They grow best, however, on rich, well-drained soils with plenty of regular rainfall.

Nearly mature fruit of either *S. mahagoni* or a hybrid, photographed in February on St. Croix; inset shows sawed-open fruit with fully developed seeds. Fruit was 3 in. (7.6 cm) long.

Uses. Both species are used for timber production. The wood is yellow-red when cut, but becomes a rich, dark brown with beautifully figured grain, and is easy to work. *Swietenia mahagoni* wood is reportedly somewhat more valuable, in part because it is less variable. The hybrids seem to have wood more similar to that of *S. mahagoni*. The trees are plantation-grown in the American tropics. Both mahoganies are widely planted for shade and as street trees, but they need a lot of room because of their aggressive root systems. Decoctions of the bark and leaves have been used to treat diarrhea, dysentery, toothache, nerve disorders, anemia, fever, and colds. Rum extract of bark is said to be an aphrodisiac, and a water extract of the bark reportedly has abortifacient properties.

Tamarindus indica L.

tamarind, *tamarindo, tamarinier*

Fabaceae (pea family)

Fruit-laden, open-grown tree in May on the grounds of the Whim Plantation Museum on St. Croix. This tree was approximately 45 ft. (14 m) tall and 53 in. (135 cm) in dbh.

A native of the African tropics, tamarind was introduced so long ago into India that it was erroneously given the specific name *indica* by botanists. Tamarind is one of the most widely planted and valued tropical fruit trees in the world, having apparently been introduced to tropical America in the 1500s. It is identified by its (1) gray-green, pinnately compound leaves; (2) beautiful flowers on long hanging stalks; (3) persisting, characteristic seed pods; and (4) large, spreading, dense crown atop a stout trunk. It is usually evergreen but can lose its leaves in particularly dry periods. It is common in the V.I., where it has escaped from cultivation, and fairly common in south Florida.

Form. Tamarind attains heights of up to 80 ft. (24 m) or more, a crown spread of 40 ft. (12 m) or more, and a trunk diameter to 8 ft. (2.4 m). The supple branches begin several feet above the ground and droop as they grow. The crown is rounded and fairly dense.

1 in.
2.5 cm

Leaves and bark. Leaves are alternate, 2–6 in. (5–15 cm) long, with 10–20 pairs of leaflets. These are 0.5–1 in. (1.3–2.5 cm) long. They close to the midrib at night and in heavy weather. The bark is very rough, fissured both vertically and horizontally.

Flowers are yellow with red accents, abundant and showy in spring, but appearing also during summer and into the fall and winter.

Fruits are heavy velvety pods, green, becoming tan when mature. They are up to 7 in. (18 cm) long, 1 in. (2.5 cm) wide and 0.5 in. (1.3 cm) thick, slightly curved, and somewhat constricted between the seeds. When mature and dry, their papery shell encloses a dark reddish-brown, sticky, sugar- and acid-laden edible pulp with several almost square, flattened brown seeds. The pods do not split open.

Clusters of flowers and buds in a crown; photographed in January on St. Croix. Inset shows a close-up of flowers, about 1 in. (2.5 cm) across.

Habitat. Tamarind trees are often seen isolated in fields—"agricultural savannas." They prefer full sun, tolerate a wide variety of soils, and are drought- and wind-tolerant. Because they are also fairly salt-tolerant, they can be grown just inland from the sea.

1 in.
2.5 cm

Uses. *Tamarindus indica* is planted for its pleasing appearance, its shade, and for its pleasant-tasting abundant fruit. The fruit is processed and used in a variety of

Open, mature fruit, photographed in March on St. John.

products, from soft drinks to Angostura bitters, Worcestershire sauce, chutneys, and many other foods. The mature seed pods are sometimes found in North American markets. Flowers, young leaves, and boiled or roasted seeds are eaten in some areas. Tamarind is used in many folk and official medicines. The fruit pulp is used as a digestive aid, laxative, and for bile disorders, to name a few. Various extracts have been used for treating asthma, digestive tract ailments, throat infections, intestinal worms,

Single pod in crown in January, St. Croix.

constipation, rheumatism, eye infections, boils, hemorrhoids, and even leprosy. Tamarind wood has dark purple-brown heartwood. It is used in general construction and to make many products in various parts of the world, from furniture and boats to turnery and tool handles. It is durable, except to drywood termites. Its density makes it a good fuel- and charcoal wood.

Tecoma stans (L.) A. Juss. ex Kunth

ginger-thomas, yellow-elder, yellow trumpetbush, *roble amarillo, esperanza, bois fleurs jaunes,* and many other names

Bignoniaceae (bignonia, catalpa family)

Nicely formed multi-stemmed tree, about 20 ft. (6 m) tall on the St. Croix campus of the University of the Virgin Islands in February. Each stem was about 5 in. (13 cm) in dbh.

Ginger-thomas is the official territorial flower of the U.S.V.I., as well as the Bahamas. This common tree or shrub is recognized by its (1) terminal clusters of beautiful yellow flowers, present nearly all year; (2) persisting long string bean-like seed pods; and (3) showy, light green, pinnately compound leaves, almost always present in south Florida and the V.I.; the tree loses its leaves in more northerly climes. *Tecoma stans* is native to the West Indies and to tropical and subtropical America, including south Texas. There seems to be some disagreement as to whether it is native to south Florida, but it is common and reproduces. It has been planted in many of the world's tropics as an ornamental.

Form is variable. Usually this tree or large shrub has multiple stems, but can be pruned to have only one. It can become 30 ft. tall (9 m), 30 ft. across the crown, and 10 in. (25 cm) in trunk diameter. The crown is fairly dense, rounded, or when multi-stemmed, has multiple rounded lobes. Branches droop with the weight of flowers and fruit.

Leaves and bark. Leaves are an attractive green above and below, 4–10 in. (10–25 cm) long. The 5–13 leaflets have toothed edges, and are 1.5–4 in. (4–10 cm) long. Bark is gray and prominently fissured.

These leaves were about 6 in. (15 cm) long.

Flowers, most abundant in the spring, occur in clusters on short stalks along a central stem. Flowers are about 1.75 in. (4.4 cm) long and 1.5 in. (4 cm) across.

Fruits. Flowers give rise to pods 4–8 in. long by 0.25 in. diameter (10–20 x 0.6 cm) in clusters. These are green, turning brown at maturity and splitting open to release numerous small seeds, in pairs with two transparent papery wings.

Flowers were about 1.75 in. (4.4 cm) across.

Habitat. A hardy plant, ginger-thomas tolerates various soils, including those dominated by rocks and/or sand. It prefers full sun, and can tolerate drought quite well and wind moderately well. It is not especially salt-tolerant, however, so is not found near the sea.

Uses. Ginger-thomas is a highly regarded native ornamental, a common landscape plant in the V.I. Extracts of its leaves, bark, and roots contain many biologically active chemicals, and have been used for treating intestinal worms, diabetes, colds, headaches, jaundice, digestive problems, yeast infections, and even syphilis. The trunk is usually too small for its wood to be useful.

Pods in the tree averaged about 6 in. (15 cm) in length. It is common to find immature and mature pods as well as flowers at the same time on the same tree.

Zanthoxylum martinicense (Lam.) DC.

white-prickle, Martinique prickly ash, *espino rubial, l'épine jaune*

Rutaceae (rue family)

Well-formed tree at St. George Village Botanical Garden, St. Croix in May. About 50 ft. (15 m) tall, this tree was 12 in. (30 cm) in dbh.

2 in.
5 cm

White-prickle is an attractive evergreen tree, grown in the V.I. and south Florida for shade. However, its utility is diminished by the presence of spines on the bark, limbs, and even leaves. It is identified by its (1) thick conical spines on the otherwise fairly smooth bark; (2) pinnately compound leaves; (3) small flowers in branched clusters (spring to fall); and (4) clusters of small 5-sectioned fruits (late spring to fall). The tree is native to the West Indies and down into Venezuela. It is common on St. John and Tortola, less so on the other V.I. It apparently is fairly rare in south Florida.

Form. *Zanthoxylum martinicense* can become 66 ft. (20 m) tall, with trunk diameter to 18 in. (46 cm). It usually has a single trunk, and has a thin, spreading crown. Large trees develop prominent buttresses.

Leaves are alternate, 6–12 in. (15–30 cm) long, with dark green, finely wavy-edged leaflets, and with hairy and often spiny midribs. Leaflets vary from 7 to 19 per leaf, and from 1.5–5 in. (4-13 cm) long.

Leaves on a twig in February on St. Croix; leaves were about 12 in. (30 cm) long. Inset shows leaflet spine.

Flower clusters are lateral and terminal, 2–6 in. (5–15 cm) long. Individual flowers are greenish-white, about 0.2 in. (0.5 cm) long and broad. Male and female flowers are on separate trees, male flowers being distinguished by having 5 protruding stamens.

Fruits are about 0.25 in. (0.6 cm) in diameter. When mature and dry, they split open into 5 parts, each with a single round seed about 0.1 in. (0.3 cm) in diameter.

Cluster of female flowers in May, each about 0.2 in. (0.5 cm) across.

Habitat. White-prickle is commonly found in moist areas in limestone-derived soils. It prefers full sun, and apparently is not especially drought-, wind-, or salt-tolerant.

Uses. The wood of *Z. martinicense* is various shades of yellow (the origin of the genus name), with heartwood sometimes being almost maroon. It has clear growth rings, but is plain. The wood is of medium weight and hard, difficult to dry, and not especially easy to work, but has been used in general construction and for making a variety of low-grade products. Its use is limited also by its great susceptibility to wood-destroying insects, and by the small size of remaining trees. Extracts of the bark and leaves have been used in numerous folk medicines for treatment of diverse ailments, from toothache and digestive disorders to venereal ulcers.

Immature fruit cluster at a twig end, photographed in May on St. Croix. Inset shows husks of mature fruit in November; their diameter was about 0.3 in. (0.8 cm).

Leaves compound, bipinnate

Compound bipinnate or twice-pinnate leaves have pinnately compound leaflets along the main leaf petiole/midrib. Sometimes it is not obvious that leaves are bipinnate, as illustrated on the facing page with the image of *Pithecellobium unguis-cati* (bread-and-cheese). In some cases it is practically impossible to tell that a leaf is bipinnate, as is the case with leaves of *Parkinsonia aculeata* (Jerusalem-thorn; included in the "Easily Recognized Trees" section and not in this section). All of the bipinnately compound leaves in this book are alternate.

Delonix regia (flamboyant-tree)

Albizia lebbeck (woman's tongue)

Pithecellobium unguis-cati
(bread-and-cheese)

Acacia macracantha Humb. & Bonpl. Ex Willd.

casha, stink casha, porknut, *tamarindo silvestre, acacia piquant*

Acacia tortuosa (L.) Willd.

casha, twisted acacia, *pomponax, aromo, pompons jaunes*

Fabaceae (pea family)

A rather large fallen casha at Haulover Bay, St. John, in May. This is *A. macracantha*, approximately 16 ft. (5 m) tall; the diameter of the largest trunk (on right) was about 12 in. (30 cm) below the fork.

Both of these acacias are common members—sometimes the dominant members—of the thorn scrub or thorn woodland ecosystems of dry habitats, such as the east ends of the Virgin Islands. The two species are similar, so they are treated together here under the common V.I. name "casha." They are identified by their: (1) evergreen foliage of feathery, small leaves; (2) small, fluffy globular clusters of yellow to orange flowers; (3) persisting seed pods; and (4) brutal thorns in pairs at leaf bases. Even goats ignore the foliage because of the thorns. The acacias bloom and bear fruit all year. Both acacia species are native to the V.I. They can be distinguished, if one desires, by the larger leaves of *A. macracantha*, the usually larger, white-tipped spines of *A. tortuosa*, and the long cylindrical pods of *A. tortuosa* as opposed to the somewhat flattened pods of *A. macracantha*. These trees or large bushes are native to the V.I. and found throughout the West Indies and down into northern South America. *Acacia macracantha* is native to south Florida; *A. tortuosa* can be found, but is rare. Several other species of acacias are found in the V.I. and south Florida, mostly as shrubs; some are similar to the two here.

Form. Cashas often have multiple trunks arising near the ground. They can become 20–30 ft. (6–9 m) tall, *A. macracantha* becoming taller. Both can have trunk diameters up to 12 in. (30 cm). Their crowns are delicate-looking, feathery, and fairly thin. Twigs are zigzag in shape, with leaves and paired thorns at the nodes.

Leaves and bark. Leaves are alternate, bipinnately compound, 1–2 in. (2.5–5 cm) long (*A. tortuosa*), and 3–6 in. (8–15 cm) long (*A. macracantha*). *Acacia macracantha* has 10–25 pairs of lateral midribs with 12–30 pairs of minute leaflets; *A. tortuosa* has 2–8 pairs of lateral midribs and 10–20 pairs of tiny leaflets. Leaves of both species are a pleasing Kelly-green color above and duller below. Bark is finely fissured on older trunks, whereas younger trunks are fairly smooth but with prominent horizontal lenticels.

Twig of *A. macracantha* showing leaves, flower buds, flower clusters, and thorns.

Flowers are in tight clusters that are about 0.4 in. (1 cm) in diameter on stalks 0.5–1 in. (1.3–2.5 cm) long, longer in *A. macracantha*. Each cluster is made up of very small, stamen-dominated, funnel-shaped flowers, fragrant in both species.

Fruit pods are 2–4 in. (5–10 cm) long and about 0.5 in. (1.3 cm) wide in *A. macracantha*, and 3–5.5 in. (7.6–14 cm) long and 0.3 in. (0.8 cm) in diameter in *A. tortuosa*. In both species the green pods turn brown to reddish-brown to almost black when mature. Mature pods do not split open and are relished by cattle and goats, which spread the small, dark brown seeds.

Habitat. Both species are found in rocky soils, often with cacti. They are drought-, salt-, and wind-resistant, and thus occupy niches with few other tree species. They often form thickets.

Uses. Cashas reportedly have very durable wood. The stems are used as fenceposts, and the wood in construction. The wood is dense and heavy, making it useful for charcoal production. Roots are nodulated with nitrogen-fixing bacteria, so the trees enrich soils. Extracts of the roots, leaves, and bark of these acacias reportedly have been used to treat hernias, inflammations, diarrhea, gangrene, and "abundant menses."

Pods of *A. tortuosa* in foliage, showing nearly mature pods; inset shows mature pods and seeds. Pods in tree were about 6 in. (15 cm) long.

Albizia lebbeck (L.) Benth.

woman's tongue, cabbagebark tree, tibet, lebbek, kokko, sirris, *acacia amarillo, arbre à graines réglisse*

Fabaceae (pea family)

Well-formed *A. lebbeck* on the Buccaneer Hotel grounds, St. Croix, in February. This tree was about 45 ft. (13.7 m) tall and had a diameter near the ground of 39 in. (99 cm).

The dry seed pods persisting on the trees of woman's tongue rattle in the tropical breezes. The tree is identified by its: (1) bipinnately compound leaves; (2) clusters of showy greenish-white flowers; and (3) persistent seed pods, which cling to the tree in clusters even when leaves are absent in the winter. The otherwise hardy tree suffers from brittle limbs and a shallow root system, making it susceptible to wind damage. Woman's tongue is not a native species, having originated in tropical Asia, but has been widely planted for shade, its showy flowers, its drought- and salt-tolerance and rapid growth. The tree is common in south Florida and on St. Croix, St. Thomas, and Tortola, but less so on St. John and Virgin Gorda. It has escaped cultivation in all these areas.

Form. *Albizia lebbeck* has a single trunk and a spreading crown. It can reach heights of 90 ft. (27 m) and trunk diameters of 36 in. (91 cm) under favorable conditions. The tree resembles the raintree (*Samanea saman*), but is readily distinguished by its leaves, flowers, and pods.

Leaves are alternate, 6–16 in. (15–41 cm) long and have 2–4 pairs of primary leaflets, each bearing 4–9 pairs of secondary leaflets. The latter are 0.75–1.75 in. (2–4.5 cm) long, rounded at both ends, and with an off-center central vein. The tree loses its leaves in the winter.

Leaf photographed in May on St. Croix.

Flower clusters resemble pompoms and are borne April to September. The individual clusters, each about 2 in. (5 cm) across, are at the ends of 1.5–4 in. (4–10 cm) stalks. They actually consist of many short-stalked flowers with long, white, protruding stamens that turn yellow and wilt with age.

Flower photographed in May on St. Croix.

Fruits. The flat seed pods, 4–8 in. (10–20 cm) long and 1–1.5 in. (2.5–4 cm) wide, are pointed at both ends and contain a row of several seeds, each about 0.4 in. (1 cm) long. Pods are produced in large numbers and dry to a tan color.

Habitat. *Albizia lebbeck* grows in full sunlight, in a variety of soils and in sand, and is often found along dry creek beds ("guts") and savannahs. It is salt- and drought-tolerant, and can be grown near the sea.

Fruit pods photographed in January on St. Croix.

Uses. In addition to its use as a landscape plant, *A. lebbeck* is a valued timber tree, although it is not grown widely for that purpose. The wood resembles that of black walnut. The roots of woman's tongue are nodulated with nitrogen-fixing bacteria, and thus improve the soil. It is planted to provide shade needed for coffee and cocoa cultivation. Leaves can be used as fodder. Bark extracts have been used to tan hides. Preparations of various parts of the tree have been used in folk medicine to treat abdominal tumors, boils, cough, lung problems, flu, boils, and other ailments. The seed oil has been used to treat leprosy.

Note: extracts of woman's tongue contain toxic chemicals.

Caesalpinia coriaria (Jacq.) Willd.

dividivi, *guatapaná, dividivi*

Fabaceae (pea family)

Well-formed dividivi in February at the St. George Village Botanical Garden, St. Croix. The tree was about 20 ft. (6 m) tall and each trunk was about 7 in. (18 cm) in diameter.

On very windy sites, this small tree grows to the leeward side in an artistic and characteristic manner. Often photographed, the official tree of Curaçao is identified by its (1) delicate, bipinnately compound leaves; (2) hard, curled or S-shaped pods, which do not open and which persist on the tree for some time after maturing; (3) dense crown composed of a mass of branching limbs; and (4) absence of thorns. When present (spring to summer), its lateral clusters of small, fragrant, light yellow pea blossom–like flowers aid in identification. Dividivi is widely distributed in the West Indies and other parts of tropical America. It is found but not especially common in the U.S.V.I., but apparently is absent from the B.V.I. and south Florida. Fine specimens are found at the St. George Village Botanical Garden on St. Croix. The species is native to the Greater Antilles, Mexico, and other tropical American regions, and perhaps to St. Croix.

Form. Dividivi attains heights of about 25–30 ft. (7–9 m) and trunk diameters of about 12 in. (30 cm) on protected sites, where it has a nicely rounded, broad, and often flat-topped crown. The tree usually branches near the ground. On windy sites, dividivi can be practically prone.

Leaves and bark. Leaves are alternate, 2–6 in. (5–15 cm) long overall. The 9–17 secondary midribs each bear 16–24 pairs of tiny leaflets about 0.2 in. (0.5 cm) long. The gray-brown bark is rough, fissured, and somewhat scaly.

Leaves and a pod in crown in February.

Flowers occur in branching lateral clusters 0.75–2 in. (2–5 cm) long, arising from leaf bases. Individual flowers, on short stalks about 0.25 in. (0.6 cm) long and broad, are comprised of five tiny petals surrounding ten stamens.

Fruit. The fruit is a tough pod about 1–2 in. (2.5–5 cm) long and 1 in. wide that contains only a few rounded seeds about 0.25 in. (0.6 cm) long. The pods do not open.

Habitat. *Caesalpinia coriaria* is drought- and wind-resistant and fairly salt-tolerant, so it grows in windy seaside areas. It tolerates a variety of soils.

Single leaf and pod.

Uses. Dividivi is used as an ornamental both in seaside areas and on protected sites. Its seed pods, 30–40% by weight tannin, are harvested and sold to make a tanning agent over some of its range. Single trees reportedly can yield 80 lbs. (36 kg) of tannin. The pods also yield a black dye, and folk medicines have been produced from them to treat fever, skin diseases, wounds, acute stomachache, and sore throat. The flowers attract bees. The wood is attractive, very heavy and hard, like that of lignum vitae. It is sometimes used in turnings, but is difficult to work. As a legume, dividivi probably harbors nitrogen-fixing bacteria in its roots (as do other *Caesalpinia* spp.), thus enriching the soil.

Flower cluster in November.

Delonix regia (Bojer ex Hook.) Raf.

flamboyant-tree, royal poinciana, *flamboyánt, flamboyant*

Fabaceae (pea family)

Flowering flamboyant, just leafing out, on the grounds of Caneel Bay resort, St. John, in May. This tree was about 18 ft. (5 m) tall, with a lower trunk diameter over 20 in. (61 cm), and a crown spread of about 40 ft. (12 m).

Flamboyant-tree is one of the most widely planted trees in the tropics around the world. Some consider it one of the world's prettiest trees when in full bloom. A native of Madagascar, it is common on most of the West Indian islands, Sometimes it escapes from cultivation, but is not generally considered a nuisance. It is easily recognized by its (1) masses of flowers; (2) large, feathery, bipinnately compound leaves, (3) distinctive form; and (4) persistent, very large seed pods, present even after leaf fall in the winter. The tree is common on all the Virgin Islands, though perhaps less so on St. Croix. It is readily found in south Florida.

Form. *Delonix regia* can grow to 50 ft. (15 m) tall and achieve a trunk diameter of more than 24 in. (61 cm). It is almost always broader than tall, and has a characteristic flattened top. When in leaf the crown is fairly dense.

Leaves and bark. Leaves are 8–20 in. (20–51 cm) long, alternate, with even-numbered feathery secondary midribs, each 2–5 in. (5–13 cm) long, and each with an even number of tiny leaflets. A single leaf may have 1,000 leaflets. The bark is mostly smooth, gray-brown, with many dots (lenticels).

10 in.
25 cm

Flowers occur from May to August in clusters borne laterally near the twig ends. Each flower is 4–5 in. (10–13 cm) across, red-orange to scarlet or occasionally yellow (perhaps a related species). The five unequal petals, to 2 in. (5 cm) long, are borne on a slender stalk, also about 2 in. long. Four of the petals have the solid color while the fifth is whitish with red-orange streaks or spots. Flowers contain both male and female parts.

1 in.
2.5 cm

Fruits. Seed pods rapidly reach large size (14–20 in. (36–51 cm) long and about 2 in. (5 cm) wide). At maturity they turn brown and are very tough, but eventually split open to release mottled brown seeds from horizontal chambers.

1 in.
2.5 cm

Habitat. Flamboyant-tree prefers full sun and tolerates a wide variety of soil types if well drained. It has high drought-tolerance but only moderate resistance to salt, and little to high winds. It seems to thrive in most habitats in the V.I. and south Florida, except right on the beaches.

Uses. The tree is widely planted for its beauty and shade, although when bare, has little of either. Its roots fix atmospheric nitrogen, enriching the soil. However, flamboyant-tree has some drawbacks. Its aggressive surface roots and buttresses can buckle walls, sidewalks, etc., and its roots can damage cisterns and swimming pools. Its fallen seed pods create a clutter, and its wood, though hard and heavy, is brittle and a favorite of termites, whose nests are common in the tree. Extracts of tree parts have been used in treatments of malaria, constipation, and bacterial infections, and reportedly have antifungal activity.

Leucaena leucocephala (Lam.) deWit.

tan-tan, wild tamarind, leadtree, *zarcilla, bois-lolo, macata* (and many more)

Fabaceae (pea family)

Open-grown tan-tan—an unusual sight—on the U.S.D.A grounds, south of Queen Mary Highway, St. Croix. Inset shows a more common appearance of this tree—as a member of an impenetrable thicket (on a hillside above Cane Bay, St. Croix). The open-grown tree was 25 ft. (7.5 m) tall and about 5 in. (13 cm) in trunk diameter at the base.

Tan-tan is probably the most common tree in the Virgin Islands, due to its prodigious powers of reproduction. Apparently a native of Mexico, it was introduced long ago throughout the tropics, including the V.I., as a cattle feed plant. It might have been introduced accidentally to Florida. In the V.I. and south Florida, it has become naturalized and proliferates with few natural enemies. Although it has some redeeming features (see Uses), its reputation in the V.I. and south Florida is not good. The small evergreen tree, usually in thickets and along roadsides, is identified from its (1) feathery bipinnately compound leaves; (2) pinkish-white spherical clusters of tiny flowers; and (3) copious clusters of pods in all stages of maturity, from green to brown. Flowers and pods are present all year.

Form. Tan-tan thickets are made up of crowded small diameter trees usually about 15–20 ft. (4.6–6 m) tall with wandlike limbs. Open-grown specimens can reach 33 ft. (10 m) in height and trunk diameters of over 5 in. (13 cm), with a spreading crown.

Leaves and bark. Leaves are alternate, 4–8 in. (10–20 cm) long. Three to 10 pairs of secondary midribs off the main midrib each have 10–20 pairs of narrow stalkless leaflets about 0.5 in. (1.3 cm) long. The leaflets close upward at night. The bark is brownish, fissured to reveal reddish underlayers, and has many lenticels.

Flowers are clustered in delicate pincushion-like but soft globes about an inch in diameter. Clusters are borne terminally or laterally on stalks about 1 in. (2.5 cm) long. Each individual flower is tubular, about 0.25 in. (0.6 cm) long, with protruding threadlike stamens.

Fruits are stalked clusters of thin 4–6 in. (10–15 cm)-long pods, green turning brown when mature and splitting open along both sides to release small, dark brown, flattened seeds.

Habitat. *Leucaena leucocephala* is a primary invader/colonizer of cut-over and degraded land. It tolerates a variety of well-drained soils, and is very salt-, drought-, and wind-resistant. Along some roadsides it must be cut back frequently so traffic can get by.

Uses. Tan-tan has a variety of uses, and is widely planted in some areas of the Old World tropics. The unripe pods and seeds are eaten as a vegetable in Mexico, Central America, and Asia. In Hawaii and many other areas, the leaves and pods are used as cattle feed. The tree is planted to rejuvenate degraded sites because its roots fix atmospheric nitrogen and it tolerates harsh conditions. The wood is hard and heavy and is used to make flooring in the Philippines, sold as "Giant ipil" wood. The seeds contain a toxin, mimosine, which, when eaten by horses and related animals, and by pigs and rabbits, causes their

hair to fall out. Cattle, sheep, and goats are unaffected. In Latin America, the bark is eaten for internal pain, and decoctions of the roots, twigs, and bark are used as contraceptives, for hair removal, and to treat back pain, menstrual cramps, fever, whooping cough, and even typhoid.

Melia azedarach L.

chinaberry, lilac, umbrella-tree, *alelaila, le lilas des Indes*

Meliaceae (mahogany family)

A nicely formed tree, even though it is a sprout from an old stump. It was about 25 ft. (7.5 m) tall and 5 in. (13 cm) in dbh. The old stump was perhaps 25 in. (64 cm) in basal diameter. Photos by Thomas Miller, taken in August in Gainesville, Florida.

Chinaberry is a common shrub or small tree, introduced to the V.I., south Florida, and elsewhere because of its pretty clusters of showy violet-purple flowers and its dark foliage. It is readily identified by its (1) bipinnately or sometimes tripinnately compound leaves, with toothed leaflets; (2) dark reddish-brown bark; (3) clusters of round fruits, green, becoming yellow and wrinkled; and, when present, (4) flowers. The tree originated in Asia, but has been widely planted around the world, escaping in most places. It is found throughout the southern U.S. as far north as Virginia, and in the west up to Washington state. In many places, including the V.I., it is considered an invasive weed tree. It is fairly common in the V.I., with the exception of St. John, and is common in south Florida.

Form. Chinaberry is usually a small, gangly tree, but can reach 50 ft. (15 m) in height and 24 in. (61 cm) in trunk diameter. Its limbs are brittle, so it frequently shows asymmetry, multiple stems, and wear due to breakage.

Leaves and bark. Leaves are alternate, 8–20 in. (20–51 cm) in overall length, with thin secondary midribs coming off the primary midrib, also thin. The narrow leaflets are 1–2 in. (2.5–5 cm) long. The bark is smooth at first, becoming furrowed with age.

Flowers and leaves in a crown on St. John in May; inset shows a single partially tripinnate leaf about 18 in. (46 cm) long.

Flowers are in clusters 4–8 in. (10–20 cm) long. Individual flowers are about 0.5 in. (1.3 cm) long and 0.75 in. (2 cm) across, on long stems. They have curved-back white petals (violet before opening), with a deep purple central column and yellow center.

Fruits are clusters of long-stemmed round "berries" that persist after leaf-fall. When old, wrinkled ones are crushed, they have an unpleasant odor. They are a little more than 0.5 in. (0.7 cm) in diameter, each with a single hard pit containing up to five seeds.

Close-up of flowers, each about 0.75 in. (2 cm) in length and width.

Habitat. *Melia azedarach* grows in a variety of soil types and climatic conditions. It prefers full sun, and has high salt- and drought-tolerance but low wind- and flood-resistance.

Uses. Various extracts of chinaberry tree parts have long been used in the East for folk medicine, including as an abortifacient, antiseptic, purgative, diuretic, and antihelmitic agent, and for fever and rheumatism. Modern studies have identified a variety of bioactive chemicals, including some with insecticidal properties, and at the time of writing these were under active investigation. The berries are not toxic to birds, which relish them and spread seeds. Though brittle, the heartwood is attractive and is used to some extent in cabinetry, etc. Because of its invasiveness, chinaberry is not often recommended for horticultural plantings.

Nearly ripe fruit clusters, photographed in August in Gainesville, Florida, by Thomas Miller.

Note: It should be noted that all parts of the tree are toxic to humans and other mammals, and serious consequences of ingestion have been reported.

Peltophorum pterocarpum (DC) Back. & Heyne

yellow flamboyant, yellow poinciana, copper pod, *flamboyán amarillo, palissandre*

Fabaceae (pea family)

Attractive tree in bloom in May at Magens Beach, St. Thomas. This tree was about 40 ft. (12 m) tall and 31 in. (79 cm) in diameter below the branch point.

A beautiful tree from tropical Asia and Australia, yellow flamboyant is planted as an ornamental in the V.I. and south Florida. Its form and bipinnately compound leaves resemble those of flamboyant (hence the name), but it is readily distinguished by its leaves, flowers, and pods. The tree is identified by its (1) large leaves (with leaflets larger than those of flamboyant); (2) large clusters of copper-colored buds opening to yellow flowers (April–Sept.); and (3) persisting clusters of flat seed pods, which turn from green to purple to tan. The tree is found along roadsides, along streets, and in yards and public parks. Though striking, is not particularly common on the major Virgin Islands or south Florida.

Form. Yellow flamboyant has a dense, spreading crown, and sometimes has multiple trunks. Trees may attain heights of 80 ft. (24 m) or more and trunk diameters of 18 in. (46 cm) or more. Twigs are rust-colored and covered with fine hairs.

Leaves and bark. Leaves are alternate and 8–16 in. (20–41 cm) long. They are feathery and delicate-looking, with their numerous leaflets 0.5–0.75 in. (1.3–2 cm) long. Like leaves of flamboyant, most are shed in the winter, but new, reddish leaves soon follow, turning yellow-green and then green. The bark is smooth with many lenticels on young trunks, but becomes fairly deeply furrowed with age.

Leaves and flower and bud cluster in crown; insets show leaf and flower detail. Flowers about 1 in. (2.5 cm) across.

Flowers. Flower buds occur in broad conical, long (to 18 in., 46 cm), terminal upright clusters along a central stem. They open from the cluster base in succession. Individual flowers have five bright yellow petals about 0.75 in. (2 cm) long, with a hairy brown stripe on the outside. Ten long stamens with

Colorful clusters of pods in crown; inset shows mature pod and seed.

orange tips protrude from flower centers. Spent flowers fall to the ground, creating a yellow carpet; trees remain almost solid yellow for weeks. Flowers have a pleasant grapelike odor.

Fruits. The flat pods are smooth, 2–4 in. (5–10 cm) long, and occur in clusters at branch ends. They persist and do not split open. Each contains 1–4 flat seeds.

Habitat *Peltophorum pterocarpum* prefers full sun and does well on dry or moist sites and in a variety of soils. It has good drought- and salt-tolerance, but its brittle branches and shallow roots give it little wind-resistance. In its northern range in Florida, it tolerates temperatures in the 20s.

Uses. This tree is widely used as an ornamental in tropical America and the West Indies. The brown, attractive wood is used in cabinetry in India. Also, in Asia, extracts of plant parts are used in folk medicines, including treatments of intestinal disorders after childbirth, sprains and bruises, and muscular pains. Bark extract is used to produce a brown dye called "soga," used with batik. The bark tannin is used to tan hides.

Pithecellobium unguis-cati (L.) Benth.

bread-and-cheese, catclaw, cat's claw, black bead, *uña de gato,
collier-diable, diaballe*

Fabaceae (pea family)

Multi-stemmed, relatively large specimen in May on the grounds of the Whim Museum, St. Croix. The largest stem was 8 in. (20 cm) in dbh, and the tree stood 32 ft. (10 m) tall.

The name "catclaw," reflected in the Latin specific name, seems a better one for this thorny tree than "bread-and-cheese." The latter term is a local expletive in the V.I., used with this tree because of its thorns and the difficulty of getting rid of it. Bread-and-cheese is the name commonly used in the V.I., whereas "cat's claw" and "black bead" are used in south Florida. The tree is recognized by its (1) paired thorns to 0.5 in. (1.3 cm) long, on the twigs among the leaves; (2) unusual bipinnately compound leaves; (3) small, delicate balls of clustered greenish to pink flowers; and (4) curled and twisted seed pods, green becoming red at maturity. Flowers and pods are seen intermittently through the year. Bread-and-cheese is an evergreen tree native to the V.I. and the other West Indian islands as well as south Florida, Mexico, Venezuela, and Guyana. It is common on all the major Virgin Islands and south Florida.

Form. Usually bread-and-cheese has multiple trunks with a dense, irregular crown. It attains heights to 30 ft. (9 m) or more, and trunk diameters of 8 in. (20 cm) or more. It occasionally forms thickets.

Leaves and bark. *Pithecellobium unguis-cati* has alternate leaves; the fact that they are bipinnately compound is not readily apparent because there are only 4 leaflets. Overall, the leaves are 1–3 in. (2.5–7.6 cm) long with very slender petioles to 1.5 in. (4 cm) long. The leaflets are stalkless, 0.5–2 in. (1.3–5 cm) long and 0.4–1 in. (1–2.5 cm) wide, smooth-margined, dark, dull green with raised veins above, and blue-green below.

Flowers occur terminally and laterally in heads about 1 in. (2.5 cm) in diameter. They are greenish-white, yellow, or pink. Individual flowers are tubular, about 0.5 in. (1.3 cm) long, on long, slender branching stalks. Male and female organs occur in the same flower.

Fruits are 2–5 in. (5–13 cm) long, curved or coiled pods. They split open on both sides to reveal shiny, black, oblong, flattened seeds about 0.4 in. (1 cm) long. These hang down from the white-to-reddish, edible pulp. The open pods persist.

Habitat. *Pithecellobium unguis-cati* is found in coastal thickets and along roadsides. It prefers full sun but tolerates moderate shade and various soils. It is drought-tolerant and moderately salt- and wind-tolerant.

Uses. Bread-and-cheese is planted as an ornamental, especially for hedges, where its thorns provide a good barrier and animals do not eat it. It responds well to pruning. The wood is light brown, hard, and heavy, and is used locally as firewood and for charcoal production. The pods are sometimes eaten as food. The seeds are used as beads in necklaces and serve as food for an endangered parrot species. Extracts of various plant parts have been used to treat fever, dysentery, kidney stones, skin infections, and—in Trinidad— to treat snake bites (fortunately, not a problem in the V.I.).

Unusual bipinnately compound leaves and thorns on twig. Leaflets were about 1 in. (2.5 cm) long; photographed in November on St. Croix.

Flower clusters photographed in February on St. Croix; clusters were about 1.25 in. (3 cm) across.

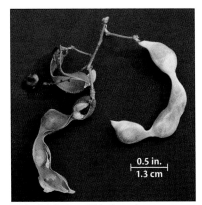

0.5 in.
1.3 cm

Colorful fruit and black seeds, photographed in May on St. Croix.

Samanea saman (Jacq.) Merr.
raintree, licorice, *samán, samana*

Fabaceae (pea family)

Young tree on the grounds of the Carambola Beach Resort in northwest St. Croix in November. This tree was approximately 42 ft. (13 m) tall and 17 in. (43 cm) in dbh.

Raintree is a beautiful and frequently large tree, native to southern Mexico and northern South America, but widely planted and naturalized in tropical areas all over the world, including the V.I. and south Florida. It is evergreen in the V.I. and probably in south Florida. Raintree is identified by its (1) wide, umbrella-shaped crown; (2) persisting seed pods; (3) bipinnately compound leaves with an even number of secondary leaflets; and (4) when present (several times a year), abundant, beautiful pink flowers. It is called raintree for several reasons: (1) its leaflets fold up during rain, allowing

Stately 300+-year-old tree at the Lawaetz Museum grounds on St. Croix in February. This tree measured over 6 ft. (1.8 m) in diameter and 55 ft (17 m) in height.

the rain to fall through the crown; (2) falling secretions of a tiny insect feeding on new growth; (3) leaf secretions; and (4) falling spent stamens. Interestingly, a very large raintree on Tobago held the tree house in the Disney movie *Swiss Family Robinson*. Raintree is found on all the major Virgin Islands, being most common on St. Croix and Tortola. It is fairly common in south Florida.

Form. Raintree usually attains a height of 55–65 ft. (17–20 m) and trunk diameters 4 ft. (1.2 m) or more. The spreading crown is usually wider than the tree is tall. Elsewhere (e.g. Tobago and Trinidad) raintree can become 125 ft. (38 m) high, greater than 7 ft. (2.1 m) in trunk diameter, and 250 ft. (76 m) in crown spread. The trunk often branches fairly low to the ground.

Leaves and bark. Leaves are 10–16 in. (25–41 cm) long overall. The primary leaf midrib has 2–8 pairs of secondary midribs, each of which bears 6–16 pairs of leaflets. Leaflets are 1–2 in. (2.5–5 cm) long, the terminal leaflet pair usually being the longest. The bark is dark gray, rough, and furrowed.

Flowers are rounded powder-puff clusters about 2.5 in. (6.4 cm) wide, borne on relatively stout 2–4 in. (5–10 cm) stalks. Individual flowers are tubular, dominated by long, threadlike stamens—the lower half white and the upper half red—giving the flower clusters a pink appearance. They can be so abundant as to give the tree an overall pink color.

This flower was almost 3 in. (7.6 cm) across, photographed in October on St. Croix.

Fruits are lumpy pods, green becoming shiny dark brown when mature, 4–8 in. (10–20 cm) long, about 0.5 in. (1.3 cm) wide and 0.25 in. (0.6 cm) thick, with prominent seams on the edges. Each has several oblong, brownish-red seeds in a licorice-flavored edible pulp. The pods eventually split open along the seams.

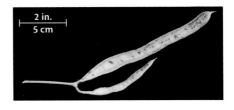

Habitat. *Samanea saman* has naturalized in low-level dry areas and savannas. It prefers full sun and can tolerate 2–4 months of drought. It grows in a variety of soil types, and is moderately salt-tolerant. The number of large trees in the V.I. suggests that it is wind-tolerant as well.

Uses. Planted mostly as a shade tree along streets and in large parks, raintree also has other uses and potential uses. The sweet pulp is eaten by animals and children, made into a refreshing drink, and has been fermented to an alcoholic beverage. The wood is soft, fairly light, but strong and resistant to decay and insects. The thin, pale sapwood surrounds the attractive brown heartwood. It is used in general construction, furniture, and a variety of other products, and in Hawaii for making "monkeypod" bowls. Raintree is an important honey plant. Extracts of the leaves, roots, and bark have been used as folk remedies for colds, diarrhea, headache, stomachaches, dermatitis, and other ailments, and the seeds chewed for sore throat. Latex from the tree has been used as glue.

Leaves compound, tripinnate

Compound tripinnate leaves have pinnately compound leaflets which themselves have pinnately compound leaflets. In this book only *Moringa oleifera* (horseradish-tree) always has tripinnately compound leaves (see image below). *Melia azedarach* (chinaberry) sometimes does (see its description on pages 164–165), but it usually has bipinnately compound leaves. The leaves of *Moringa oleifera* are alternate along the twigs.

Moringa oleifera (horseradish-tree)

Moringa oleifera Lam.

horseradish-tree, drumstick, *ben, resedá, malok*

Moringaceae (moringa family)

A clump of horseradish-trees on the campus of the University of the Virgin Islands on St. Thomas, in November. The overall height was 20 ft. (6 m) and the largest trunk had a diameter of over 8 in. (20 cm) at its base.

Horseradish-tree is an ornamental in the V.I. and south Florida, but much more than that in many parts of the world (see Uses below). It is easily identified by its (1) large, light green, tripinnately compound leaves; (2) showy clusters of cream-colored flowers, always present; and (3) large pods, green becoming brown, and also always present. Native to India, the East Indies, and Southeast Asia, *M. oleifera* has been planted in most tropical areas of the world. It is very easy to propagate, and reportedly one of the world's fastest-growing trees. It is fairly common in south Florida and on St. Croix, St. John, and Tortola, but less so on Virgin Gorda and St. Thomas. Because it has escaped cultivation and grows so fast, it may be expected to become more common.

Form. Horseradish-tree can become 33 ft. (10 m) tall and 10 in. (25 cm) or more in trunk diameter. The spreading, drooping branches are brittle, which often limits the tree's size and appearance in windy areas. It usually has a single trunk.

Leaves are alternate, 12–18 in. (30–46 cm) long overall, very pale green when young, becoming darker with age.

Flowers occur in clusters that are attached to a central flower stem. Overall, these fragrant "clusters of clusters" are 4–8 in. (10–20 cm) long. Individual flowers are fairly typical pea-blossom type in appearance.

Fruits are distinctive pods, 7–20 in. (18–51 cm) long, with nine ridges when immature and maturing to a three-angled brown pod that splits along the three angles. Each pod contains 5–20 seeds, each with three papery wings.

Habitat. *Moringa oleifera* grows in a wide variety of soil types provided they are well drained. It is extremely drought-tolerant and does quite well on dry, sandy sites. It is not very salt-tolerant, however, which means it is not found near the sea.

Uses. Horseradish-tree has an incredible variety of uses—too numerous to mention but a few here. The tree is one of the most useful plants in tropical areas—especially in dry tropics. The roots taste like horseradish and are used the same way. The immature pods ("drumsticks") are cooked and eaten like string beans (reportedly they taste like asparagus). Leaves and flowers are also eaten as vegetables and in salads, soups, and sauces. All are high in protein and vitamins A and C. Tea made from the leaves is said to energize. Preparations of the gum are used in food seasoning, and the gum and other parts of the plant in folk remedies (e.g. to treat stomach and bladder ailments, headaches, flu, sore throat, and even cancers). Crushed seeds are used to purify water (by causing particles to settle out). Seed oil ("Ben oil") is non-drying and is used as a fine lubricant. It is also used in salads and as cooking oil. The leaves and young branches make excellent forage. The trees are used as living fence posts, for windbreaks and hedges, for shade, and for fuelwood. They are good honey plants.

Leaves can be quite large; the diameter of this one was 19.5 in. (50 cm).

Individual flowers were about 0.75 in. (2 cm) across. A fruit pod is also shown.

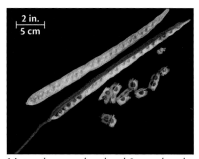

Mature large seed pod and 3-vaned seeds.

Leaves compound, palmate

Compound palmate leaves have two to several leaflets arising from the end of the petiole. Only three trees in this book have palmately compound leaves, which are shown below. *Tabebuia heterophylla* (white-cedar) has opposite leaves, whereas *Adansonia digitata* (baobab) and *Ceiba pentandra* (kapok) have alternate leaves.

Tabebuia heterophylla (white-cedar)

Adansonia digitata (baobab)

Ceiba pentandra (kapok)

Adansonia digitata L.

baobab, dead rat tree, *baobab, calebassier du Sénégal*

Bombacaceae (bombax family)

This specimen was about 45 ft. (14 m) tall and 60 in. (152 cm) in diameter, located on the grounds of the Lawaetz Museum on St. Croix. February.

10 in.
25 cm

Bark of a tree near Homestead, Florida.

Baobab is not very common in the V.I. or Florida, but is so unusual that almost anyone seeing it will want to know more about it. The tree is odd, readily identified by its: (1) very stout but short and almost columnar or even vaselike trunk; (2) relatively smooth gray bark; (3) thick primary branches; (4) palmately compound leaves; and, when present, (5) large, gourd-like fruits hanging on long stalks. A native of the dry plains and savannahs of Africa, the tree is steeped in spiritual folklore. In their dry native habitat, old, very large trees become hollow and reservoirs of water, nesting sites for bees, and even habitats for humans. There the trees can reach 30 ft. (9 m) or more in diameter, become 60 ft. (18 m) tall or taller, and live 2,000 years or longer. Baobab is therefore among the world's largest, most unusual, and longest-lived trees. In the V.I. and south Florida, trees 10 ft. (2.5 m) in diameter can be found.

Form. The massive trunk of baobab is striking. The branches usually form a medium-density canopy that is larger in diameter than the tree's height.

Leaves and bark. Baobab is unusual among V.I. and tropical Florida trees in that it has palmately compound leaves. They are alternate, with petioles 4–5 in. (10–13 cm) long and with 3–7 smooth-edged leaflets 3–6 in. (8–15 cm) long. Leaves appear after spring rains and fall during the dry season. Bark remains smooth even in old trees.

Flowers. The very large flowers—up to 12 in. (30 cm) in diameter—are another unusual feature of the baobab tree. They are not often seen because they appear only in late afternoon and at night, then turn brown and disappear the next morning. They are borne October to December, singly on long pendant stalks. The flowers are pretty, with five creamy white petals and a central yellowish, globular reproductive structure (bisexual) borne on a white tube.

Fruits, occurring on the long flower stalks, are hard, green, gourdlike structures growing to 6–12 in. (15–30 cm) long and 2–3.5 in. (5–9 cm) in diameter at maturity, when they become yellow-brown. Inside, the kidney-shaped seeds are borne in a dry mealy pulp that is sour but edible.

Habitat. Baobab grows in dry, infertile soils and tolerates drought, especially when leafless in the dry winter season. It does not tolerate shade and is not salt-tolerant. Its thick branches and open crown suggest that it is fairly wind-resistant.

Uses. Baobab has many uses involving all parts of the tree. In Africa, its bark provides fiber for rope and other cordage products. There the young leaves are cooked and

Flower and immature fruits in crown of a tree, early on a November morning, outside of St. George Village Botanical Garden, St. Croix.

eaten as an important source of food, and modern studies have shown them to be of high nutritional value. The fruit pulp, high in vitamin C, is made into a lemonade-like drink, and the seeds are ground into an edible meal. Extracts of the fruit pulp and bark are used in Africa to treat infections; to treat bladder, kidney, and liver diseases; to alleviate diarrhea; and for many other medicinal purposes. The wood is spongy and not very useful as lumber, but dugout canoes are carved from the trunks. Baobabs are used as street trees and in estates and city parks in the Old and New World tropics, especially in India and South America. There are a few fine old specimens in estates and parks in south Florida and the V.I. Baobabs are beautiful as dominant, attention-grabbing specimens, but are not for the small garden!

Adansonia digitata   179

Ceiba pentandra (L.) Gaertn.

kapok, silk-cotton-tree, jumbie tree, *ceiba, mapou*

Bombacaceae (bombax family)

Typical open-grown kapok tree at St. George Village Botanical Garden, St. Croix, in November. About 60 ft. (18 m) tall and 24 in. (61 cm) in diameter above the buttresses, this tree had a ring of epiphytes on the trunk.

12 in.
30 cm

One of the largest trees in the V.I. and south Florida, kapok is so striking that it will be remembered when encountered again. It is the producer of the kapok ("silk cotton") of commerce, and is grown on plantations for that purpose in Ceylon and Java. Kapok is identified by its (1) huge buttresses 6–12 in. (15–30 cm) thick, extending considerable distances from the trunk; (2) thick trunk and stout horizontal branches; (3) alternate, palmately compound leaves; (4) beautiful flowers at branch ends (winter); and (5) in the late winter and spring, its distinctive fruit pods, and later the silk cotton balls. Native to South America, kapok has floating seed capsules which might have been carried by sea to Africa, where it is also considered native. The tree has been widely planted elsewhere. Large specimens are found in the National Park on St. John. It is common in the V.I. and not difficult to find in south Florida.

Form. Older trees have straight, cylindrical trunks above the buttresses, with no low branches. The trees can reach 9 ft. (2.7 m) in diameter above the buttresses, and heights nearing 200 ft. (61 m) in some parts of Africa. The thin crown is frequently wider than the tree is tall.

Leaves and bark. Drooping leaflets, usually five, but sometimes six or seven, are 3–8 in. (8–20 cm) long, on slender petioles 3–9 in. (8–23 cm) long. They are shed in Nov.–Dec., with new leaves appearing in Feb.–Mar. Bark on young trees and branches is smooth and green, with stubby sharp spines. The bark on older trees is smooth and spines are gradually lost.

Leaf, photographed in January.

Flowers. Flower buds, in lateral clusters near twig ends, resemble acorns, and occur in large numbers. They open at night from November to February. The individual bisexual flowers have five waxy petals, whitish to pink, and long stamens; petals are about 1.5 in. (4 cm) long; they have brown hairs on the outer surface. Flowers have an unpleasant odor, attracting the bats that pollinate them.

Flowers in a crown, November.

Fruits. Fruit capsules are large—to 8 in. (20 cm) long and 2 in. (5 cm) in diameter—and boat-shaped. When mature, in spring and summer, they split open along five seams while still on the tree, releasing balls of "silk cotton" with numerous small pea-shaped brown seeds embedded. The balls are blown apart and dispersed by wind.

Habitat. *Ceiba pentandra* prefers full sun and coastal plains, being both drought- and salt-tolerant.

Uses. The fluffy fruit fiber is used to stuff pillows, cushions, etc., and in insulation; it was once the major material used in life preservers. Kapok wood is very lightweight, and stronger than balsa wood (which is in the same family), but it is very susceptible to stain, decay, and insect damage. Even so, it is used for lumber core stock, plywood veneer, crating, and packaging.

Immature fruit pods and new leaves in March on St. John. Insets show "silk cotton" balls from opened mature pods in May on St. John and a cut-open immature fruit.

It was used in the past to make dugout canoes. Seeds yield an oil used in soaps and cosmetics, with seed residues serving as cattle feed. Plant extracts have been used as a contraceptive and to treat dizziness, boils, upset stomach, high blood pressure, tumors, wounds, and coughs. Kapok is a striking ornamental tree where space permits (its roots will damage nearby structures), and it is a good honey tree.

Tabebuia heterophylla (DC.) Britton

white-cedar, pink-cedar, pink manjack, *robler blanco, poirier gris*

Bignoniaceae (bignonia, catalpa family)

This tree, photographed in May on the Caneel Bay resort grounds on St. John, was approximately 40 ft. (12 m) tall and 23 in. (58 cm) in dbh.

White-cedar is the official tree of the British Virgin Islands as well as Anguilla. It is a variable tree, depending on its growing site. On favorable sites, it is identified by its (1) palmately compound leaves with yellow petioles and, usually, five unequal leaflets; (2) persistent seed pods; and (3) when present (most of the year), its showy flowers. On poor sites, such as the dry areas of the V.I., the trees, leaves, and fruits are smaller, and the leaves may have only one to three leaflets. The species is native to Puerto Rico and the V.I., but not south Florida, and is found throughout the West Indies. It is common in the V.I. and widely planted as an ornamental in south Florida. It is usually evergreen, though fewer leaves are seen in the dry season. The name white-cedar refers to the tree's bark, which sometimes resembles that of cedars; there, however, the resemblance to true cedars ends.

Form. White-cedar is a small to medium-size tree growing to 60 ft. (18 m) tall and 18 in. (46 cm) in trunk diameter on good sites, where it usually has a single erect trunk and a narrow columnar crown. On poor sites, it commonly has multiple stems and an overall scraggly appearance.

Leaves are opposite, dull green, and 6–12 in. (15–30 cm) long, including the petiole, which is 2–5 in. (5–13 cm) long. Leaflets vary from 2–6 in. (5–15 cm) long.

Leaves with 2, 3, and 5 leaflets from a single tree.

Flowers occur in lateral and terminal clusters, or singularly, on slender stalks. Flowers are 2–3 in. (5–7.6 cm) across and about 3 in. (7.6 cm) long, usually deep pink with yellow centers.

Fruits are hanging pods up to 8 in. (20 cm) long, with lengthwise ridges. When mature they split open along two sides, releasing numerous small, light-brown seeds with two white wings.

Tabebuia heterophylla flower in crown, in January on St. Croix.

Habitat. White-cedar prefers full sun and tolerates a variety of soil types. It has high drought-tolerance and fairly good wind- and salt-tolerance. It is common in relatively dry, evergreen forest ecosystems.

Uses. *Tabebuia* species are among the world's most valuable timber trees. The woods of the *Tabebuias* are all very durable. In the West Indies, *T. heterophylla* wood is used for boats, flooring, cabinetry, furniture, and many other products. It is also grown as an ornamental, mainly for its beautiful flowers, which cover the whole tree in the spring. Another species, *Tabebuia aurea,* has bright yellow flowers, and is also a popular ornamental in the V.I. and south Florida.

Large clusters of *T. aurea* flowers in a crown, in May on St. Croix.

Various folk medicines have been prepared from white-cedar bark, leaves, and fruit. Tea made

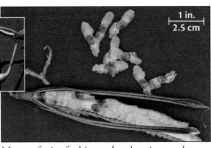

from the leaves, for example, has been used to treat bed-wetting, toothaches, backaches, gonorrhea, and fish poisoning. *Tabebuia heterophylla* is an important honey plant.

Mature fruit of white-cedar showing seeds; inset shows nearly mature, unopened fruit; photographs made in February and May (inset).

CACTUSES

Cactuses of course are distinguished by having inconspicuous or no leaves, and by having spines. Photosynthesis is carried out by the branches. The two species covered in this book are shown below and described in this section.

Consolea rubescens (tree cactus)

Pilosocereus royenii (pipe-organ cactus)

Consolea rubescens (Salm-Dyck ex DC.) Lem.

tree cactus, sour prickly pear, roadkill cactus, blydenbush, *tuna de petate, petites raquettes*

Cactaceae (cactus family)

*Consolea rubescen*s at St. George Village Botanical Garden, St. Croix, photographed in May. Plant was approximately 10 ft. (3 m) tall, and 8 in. (20 cm) in trunk diameter near the base.

Note: This species is synonymous with *Opuntia rubescens*.

One of the two cactus species reaching small tree size in the V.I., tree cactus looks more like a tree than the other one, *Pilosocereus royenii*. It is native to the V.I., and is apparently not found in south Florida. *Consolea rubescens* is identified by its (1) single trunk that is branchless for several feet and covered with long grayish-white spines; (2) stout spiny branches; (3) big flattened secondary branches; and (3) fruits and flowers on the edges of the secondary branches, most located near the ends, and found year-round. Tree cactus is common on the east ends of St. John, St. Thomas, Tortola, and Virgin Gorda; it is less common on St. Croix.

Form. This cactus can reach a height of 20 ft. (6m) or more, with a trunk diameter of 10 in. (25 cm). Its spines are 0.25–2 in. (0.6–5 cm) long, arising singly or more commonly in groups of 2–6 from central points. The form of this cactus gives it a somewhat disorganized and unkempt appearance.

Leaves and bark. Leaves are tiny and inconspicuous at the bases of the spines. Photosynthesis is carried out by the branches, which are green year-round. Bark is reddish-brown, becoming furrowed and flaky. Under the bark the inner bark is a fleshy yellowish water-storing tissue that surrounds spongy, woody tissue.

Flowers are attractive, orange, red, or yellow, about 0.75 in. (2 cm) across with overlapping petals. They are borne terminally on spiny 1.5–2 in. (4–5 cm)-long, egg-shaped tubercles, which technically are part of the flower, and which morph into the fruit.

Fruits bear many small seeds, but commonly fall to the ground and take root with seeds intact. Seeds are, however, spread by birds that eat the fruit; birds also make nest holes in the trunk.

Flowers and fruits occur together, the latter becoming purple as they ripen. The flowers were 0.75 in. (2 cm) across.

Habitat. Superbly adapted to the harshest dry parts of the V.I., tree cactus thrives with few other plant species. The plant is wind-, salt-, and drought-resistant, and apparently unconcerned about soil type.

Uses. Tree cactus stabilizes soils in desertlike areas of the V.I., and serves as a refuge for some birds. A spineless variety—and sometimes that with spines—is used as an ornamental. Several species of *Opuntia* are edible, and folk remedies have been based on extracts of plant parts. However, no specific reference of *C. rubescens* (or *O. rubescens*) in either regard was found.

Pilosocereus royenii (L.) Byles & Rowley

pipe-organ cactus, dildo, Royen's tree cactus, *sebucán, cactus cierge*

Cactaceae (cactus family)

Large old *Pilosocereus royenii* on the east end of St. Croix. This cactus was over 20 ft. (6 m) tall, and had a base diameter of nearly 3 ft. (91 cm).

Note: This cactus species has had at least 30 scientific synonyms; the one used here seems to be the currently accepted one.

Pipe-organ cactus is the most conspicuous cactus in the V.I., being found in dry areas such as the eastern ends of the islands. It is easily recognized by its (1) form; (2) relatively large size; (3) abundant clustered thorns; (4) tufts of whitish hairs near the branch ends; (5) elongated flowers; and (6) red-purple fruits. The species is found in the northern Lesser Antilles and on Puerto Rico. It is native to the V.I. and common on all the major islands. It is not native to south Florida, but Fairchild Tropical Botanic Garden in Coral Gables lists three specimens growing there.

Form. *P. royenii* has upward-reaching mostly vertical branches 2–4 in. (5–10 cm) in diameter, arising 1–2 ft. (0.3–0.6 m) above ground from a single trunk. Branches may branch again, and those yet again. Overall, this cactus may reach 20 ft. (6 m) or more in height and have a trunk diameter of 24 in. (61 cm) or larger. Each branch has 7–11 vertical ribs or ridges, with white-gray to yellow, slender, sharp spines, 0.5–2 in. (1.3–5 cm) long, arising in clusters from the ribs. Branches often have cavities about 2 in. (5 cm) in diameter—the nesting sites of small birds.

Just-opening flower, about 2.5 in. (6.3 cm) long.

Leaves and bark. The plant has no leaves; photosynthesis is carried out by the gray-green branches. Branches have thick bark, whereas the trunk bark is very thin, relatively smooth and reddish-brown.

Flowers are about 2 in. (5 cm) long and 1 in. (2.5 cm) in diameter. They are fleshy, whitish-green to purple-red. They extend horizontally out from the branches and open at night, but last into the next day. They are found year-round.

Fruits. The edible red fruit is flattened, about 2 in. (5 cm) across. It is juicy and sweet and contains many tiny black seeds. Fruits do not have spines, but getting them off the plant is a bit dicey. They are usually found year-round.

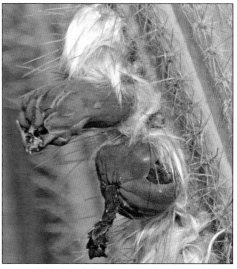

Flower (above) and fruit on St. Croix in May. Note exposed red flesh and tiny black seeds where a section of the fruit rind had been torn off. The fruit was about 2 in. (5 cm) in diameter. Tufts of white hairs are also present.

Habitat. Pipe-organ cactus prefers dry sites with full sun. It does well on poor, rocky soils, and is very drought-, wind-, and salt-tolerant.

Uses. *P. royenii* is a robust plant that helps to stabilize poor soils. It is attractive and is used in landscaping. Reports of medicinal uses were not found.

Palms

Palms characteristically have a single trunk with a grouping of leaves at the top. The leaves are usually quite large, as is the case with the five palms included in this book.

Cocos nucifera (coconut palm)

Sabal causiarum (Puerto Rican hat palm)

Coccothrinax barbadensis (Lodd. Ex Mart.) Becc.

tyre-palm, silver palm, silver thatch palm, *palma de abanico, latanier balai*

Aricaceae (palm family)

Typical skinny tyre-palm at Magens Bay, St. Thomas, in February; this tree was 45 ft. (13.7 m) tall and only 4 in. (10 cm) dbh.

Crowns blowing in the wind above the forest canopy.

This skinny palm is noticed because its crown of fan-shaped leaves sticks out above the forest canopy. In the trade winds the leaf fans expose conspicuous silvery undersides. It is identified by its (1) round leaves, split into many sections, shiny green above and dull silvery below; (2) flower clusters (May–June), much branched, attached among the leaves; and (3) many round blue-black fruits arising along a drooping stalk. Sometimes a fibrous network is seen at leaf bases. Tyre-palm is native to Puerto Rico and the V.I., and perhaps much of the rest of the Caribbean and northern South America, and was introduced into south Florida. (Several palms were previously classified as separate species, and have now been combined into *C. barbadensis*.) Tyre-palm is common on the north-facing forested hillsides of St. John, St. Thomas, and Tortola; it is less common on St. Croix, and apparently absent on Virgin Gorda; in south Florida, it is fairly common as a horticultural tree.

Form. Tyre-palm attains heights up to 50 ft. (15 m), with trunk diameters of only 2–5 in. (5–13 cm). The thin crown has 8–15 leaves.

Leaves and bark. Leaf blades in the fan are accordion-folded and leathery, tapering from about 1.5 in. (4 cm) wide to a sharp point. They are 3–4 ft. (0.9–1.2 m) in diameter and about 3.5 ft. (1.1 m) long. Older leaves become brown, droop, and eventually fall. The bark is smooth and brown, with long, vertical, shallow cracks.

This leaf was 39 in. (1 m) across.

Flower clusters are made up of many slender horizontal branches off a central stem. Individual flowers are white, stalkless, and only about 0.1 in. (0.2 cm) long and broad.

Fruits are up to 0.5 in. (1.3 cm) in diameter, with fleshy pulp containing a single seed about 0.2 in. (0.5 cm) in diameter.

Habitat. Tyre-palm is found on moist hillsides, often growing in rocky soils. It is reportedly very resistant to drought and salt, and has good wind-resistance.

Uses. This species is attractive, and is used as an ornamental. The fruit is edible, and was once (perhaps even now) used to make jam. Leaves have been used for thatching roofs. Leaf decoctions have been used to treat respiratory ailments.

Flower clusters in crown, photographed on St. John in May, were about 18 in. (46 cm) long, on stalks of about the same length.

Clusters of mature fruits in crown in February on St. Thomas.

Cocos nucifera L.

coconut, coconut palm, *palma de coco, cocotier*

Arecaceae (palm family)

Cocos nucifera tree on Magens Beach, St. Thomas, in January; the tree was about 43 ft. (13 m) tall, with a dbh of 14 in. (36 cm).

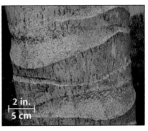

The coconut palm is one of the most valuable trees in the world, besides being a symbol of the beauty of the tropics. They are a favorite support for hammocks, but the heavy old leaves and mature fruit must be removed before they fall on a relaxed tourist. The tree is recognized by its (1) familiar large coconuts, year-round in the V.I. and south Florida; (2) new upright leaves at the top of the crown; (3) yellow and brown leaves in the lower crown; (4) bulbous enlargement at the trunk base; and (5) pendant, branched, long clusters of whitish or pale yellow flowers arising from long pointed sheaths at leaf bases. Coconut originated in the old world tropics, was brought many years ago to the Caribbean and south Florida, where it has long been naturalized. It is common. Coconut is grown commercially in many tropical areas—but not the V.I., and only to a limited extent in south Florida.

Form. Coconut trees can become 60 ft. (18 m) or more in height, and the slender trunk 8–12 in. (20–30 cm) in diameter. The tree is often leaning and curved because of wind, beach erosion, and hurricane damage.

Leaves and bark. Leaves are 12–20 ft. (3.7–6 m) long, including a 3–5 ft. (0.9–1.5 m) grooved petiole, and are 3–5 ft. (0.9–1.5 m) wide. The shiny, slender leaflets are 2–3.5 ft. (0.6–1 m) long and about 2 in. (5 cm) wide, drooping from the central leaf stem. A basal sheath, about 2 ft. (0.6 m) long, green turning to brown, surrounds the leaf base. The smooth bark is gray to brown, with small vertical cracks.

Flowers. Flower stalk branches, about 4 ft. (1.2 m) long, have numerous male flowers about 0.5 in. (1.3 cm) long and broad, and a single female flower at the base, about 3x the size of the males.

Fruits. Coconuts are green- to yellow-colored through maturity, then turn brown. They are football-shaped, 8–12 in. (20–30 cm) long, and are rounded/triangular in cross-section. The husk, about 1 in. (2.5 cm) thick, does not split open. Inside the husk is one of the world's largest seeds, the familiar fiber-covered, oblong, brown "coconut," with three dark round spots at one end—the so-called "monkey face." Inside the tough seed shell a slightly sweet, oily white meat encloses a milk-filled cavity.

Flower clusters in crown of a tree on St. Croix in March; clusters were about 36 in. (91 cm) long; inset shows close-up of individual male flowers.

Habitat. Coconut palm prefers full sun and is wind- and salt-resistant. It is found growing in sand along beaches. It is not especially drought-tolerant.

Uses. Coconut milk and the oily white meat of the seed are important foods. The dried meat, "copra," is an important product of commerce from which coconut oil is pressed. The latter is used as a food

Maturing fruits in crown, each 8–10 in. (20–25 cm) long, in May on St. Croix.

oil, but over 90% of the fatty acids are saturated. The oil is also used in cosmetics and a variety of other products. The soft jellylike immature flesh in the seed is eaten with a spoon. Raw coconut meat and milk from the mature fruit are consumed as is, and are ingredients in many dishes and drinks. Coconut fiber, "coir," is made into mats, ropes, brushes, etc. The wood of the outer part of the trunk is used for various products, but the trunk interior is too soft and spongy for most uses. Coconut wood is used for posts, firewood, light flooring, and some other construction. Because of its unusual appearance, the wood is also used to make novelties. Resin from the inner husk of coconut fruit has been used to treat toothache, and diabetics have reported improvements from consuming coconut oil. Root and bark extracts and coconut milk reportedly can be used to treat intestinal worms, fatigue, bladder infection, thrush, and many other ailments.

Phoenix canariensis hort. Chabaud

Canary Island date palm, *palmera canaria*, *dattier des Canaries*

Arecaceae (palm family)

Typical specimen in the Kopsick Palm Arboretum in St. Petersburg, Florida, in December. This flowering tree was 27 ft. (8.2 m) tall, with a dbh of 18 in. (46 cm).

Canary Island date palm is one of the most widely planted ornamentals in the tropics and subtropics around the world. It is a large, imposing tree that dominates its environment wherever it is planted. It is identified by its (1) single, upright, often very thick trunk with elongated diamond-shaped leaf scars; (2) large, rounded crown of very long leaves split between the veins into almost delicate "leaflets;" (3) large clusters of yellow dates, turning almost black, arising from leaf bases; and (4) long, sharp spines at leaf bases. It is fairly common in the V.I. and quite common in south Florida.

Form. *Phoenix canariensis* can be truly massive, with heights over 60 ft. (18 m) and trunk diameters of over 48 in. (122 cm). The trunk does not taper noticeably. The crown is made up of over 50 leaves that arch upward and outward, giving a crown diameter to over 40 ft. (12 m). Often the older leaves are cut back, leaving a bulbous section at the top of the trunk. In moist areas, the leaf crotches are often home to a wide variety of epiphytes.

Sharp spines adorn the leaf petiole bases; these spines were 3–4 in. (7.5–10 cm) long.

Leaves and bark. The evergreen leaves are arranged in a spiral manner. They have an odd number of leaflets, 12–18 in. (30–46 cm) long. The trunk bark is very rough, with the leaf scars extending all the way to the ground.

Flowers occur on branched stalks arising among the leaves and extending out and downward 36 in. (91 cm) or more. Male and female flowers occur on different trees; in both cases, the individual flowers are inconspicuous, but en masse are bright yellow.

Fruits occur in large pendant clusters on branched stalks. Individual dates are 0.5–1 in. (1.3–2.5 cm) long, olive-shaped. They become purplish-black with maturity. Although edible, they are not tasty.

Habitat. Canary Island date palm prefers full sun, has high drought- and wind-tolerance and moderate tolerance to salty air. It grows in a variety of soils.

Flower clusters and some immature fruit in crown. Photographed in May by Jozef Keularts on St. Croix.

Uses. The major use of this palm is as a very popular ornamental. Its size requires large areas, such as along boulevards and in open parks. It requires pruning to remove old fronds, which are heavy and can cause damage if allowed to fall. Wood of the tree has been used in general construction in the Canary Islands. Reportedly, the pollen (from the male trees) is a serious allergen. No reports of traditional medicinal uses were encountered.

Fruit clusters in the orange-red stage of maturity, photographed in December in Sarasota, Florida.

Roystonea borinquena O. F. Cook

Puerto Rico royal palm, mountain-cabbage, *palma real,
palmier royal de Puerto Rico*

Arecaceae (palm family)

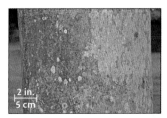

The Puerto Rico royal palm is one of the stateliest trees in the V.I. and south Florida. It is native to Puerto Rico, where it is very common, and to St. Croix, and perhaps to Tortola. It is identified by its (1) single straight trunk, with a swelling several feet up; (2) narrow green column of leaf sheaths at the top of the trunk; (3) vertical spike (the newest leaf) at the top of the tree; and (4) ever-present flowers and fruit. On St. Croix, large specimens line the entrance road to St. George Village Botanical Garden. Cuban royal palm, *Roystonia regia,* is a very similar tree, also planted in the V.I. and especially in south Florida. In *R. borinquena,* the narrow leaf segments are in a single plane, whereas in *R. regia,* the segments come

Puerto Rico royal palms at the St. George Village Botanical Garden, St. Croix, in February. The featured tree was about 55 ft. (16.8 m) tall and had a dbh of 16 in. (41 cm).

out from the midribs in several planes. *Roystonea borinquena* is common on St. Croix and Tortola, less so on the other major Virgin Islands.

Form. Puerto Rico royal palm has a distinctive straight trunk. The leaves form a rounded crown, dense near the middle.

Leaves and bark. Leaves are 8–12 ft. (2.4–3.7 m) long, with two rows of narrow sections on each side of the midrib, giving the leaves a full look. Leaf sections are 20–36 in. (51–91 cm) long and 0.75–1.75 in. (2–4.4 cm) wide, and curve downward. The bark is smooth and gray, with many faint rings of leaf scars.

Flowers are borne below the leaf sheath in twice-branched showy clusters 3–5 ft. (0.9–1.5 m) long. Male and female flowers are separate, but in the same clusters. Males are about 0.25 in. (0.6 cm) long and about 0.5 in. (1.3 cm) wide, cream-colored with purple tips. Female flowers are also cream-colored, but much smaller.

Fruits are numerous in large clusters, green-yellow at first but becoming light brown. They are shaped like small olives (0.5 in., 1.3 cm, long). Each contains a single oily seed about 0.25 in. (0.6 cm) long.

Habitat. *Roystonea borinquena* is a robust tree that fares well even along streets with limited space around the base. It tolerates a variety of soil types as long as it gets enough water. It prefers full sun, is moderately wind-resistant, but is not drought- or salt-tolerant.

Uses Puerto Rico royal palm is a landscape tree, often planted in rows along entryways and streets. It is an important source of nectar for honey bees. Its leaves, leaf sheaths, and sawn lumber have been used as sheathing and in construction, especially in Puerto Rico. In folk medicine, root decoctions have been used to treat bladder stones and diabetes, and as a diuretic.

Flower cluster in crown photographed in May on St. Croix; inset shows close-up.

Cluster of nearly mature fruits, photographed in May on St. Croix.

Sabal causiarum (O. F. Cook) Beccari

Puerto Rican hat palm, Puerto Rico palmetto, *palma de sombrero, palmier sabal*

Arecaceae (palm family)

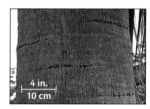

The Puerto Rican hat palm is actually used to make hats of high quality. It is native to Puerto Rico, Hispaniola, and perhaps to the V.I. It is identified by its (1) single stout trunk, columnar or tapering slightly and smooth; (2) large, blue-green, fan-shaped leaves with very long petioles that extend about half-way into the blades; (3) residual split stubs of old petioles under the existing leaves; (4) small whitish flowers in much-branched clusters on long stalks arising from leaf bases and extending beyond the leaf crown; and (5) very long clusters of small round fruits. Flowers and/or fruits can usually be seen year-round in the V.I. and south Florida. *Sabal*

Sabal causiarum at the St. George Village Botanical Garden, St. Croix in November. It was approximately 30 ft. (9 m) tall and 18 in. (46 cm) in dbh.

causiarum is a very slow-growing tree. Most specimens in the V.I. have been planted, although there are reports that it has become naturalized. It has not become naturalized in south Florida.

Form. Mature Puerto Rican hat palm has a dense, rounded crown of about 40 leaves. The trunk can have diameters up to 4 ft. (1.1 m), and the tree attains heights of 30 ft. (9.1 m) or more.

Leaves and bark. Leaf petioles are 3–8 ft. (0.9–2.4 m) long, with blades 3–6 ft. (0.9–1.8 m) in diameter. The blades are split into long, narrow segments 1.5–2 in. (4–5 cm) wide. Leaves droop as they age, turn tan-colored, and drop off. There is no "hula skirt" (as seen with other *Sabal* species). The bark is relatively smooth, with rows of horizontal "warts."

Flower clusters, on a central stalk 8–10 ft. (2.4–3 m) long, are up to 8 in. (20 cm) long, and arise from brown sheaths along the central stalk. Individual flowers are only about 0.2 in. (0.5 cm) long, stalkless, with three narrow white petals and six protruding stamens.

Leaves were about 7 ft. (2.1 m) long.

Fruits are numerous, green at first but becoming dark brown. They are shaped like small (0.5 in., 1.3 cm, long) olives. Each is borne on a small stalk, and contains a single seed about 0.4 in (1 cm) in diameter.

Habitat. *Sabal causiarum* requires full sun, grows in a variety of soil types, is salt-tolerant, wind-resistant, and, once established, drought-resistant. This palm is fairly cold-tolerant as well, surviving over-night exposure to 16°F (-9°C), so it can be grown farther north than most palms.

Young flower cluster in crown, photographed by Jozef Keularts on St. Croix in May.

Mature and immature fruits in a cluster, photographed in December on St. Croix.

Uses. For use in making hats, the leaves are boiled, dried, and bleached. Leaves are also used as thatch. The trees are planted in Puerto Rico as ornamentals and for their leaves. In the V.I. and south Florida, they are imposing, large trees—too large for most yards. No references to folk medicinal uses of this tree were found.

Veitchia merrillii (Beccari) H. E. Moore

Christmas palm, Manilla palm, *adonidia, palmier de Noël*

Arecaceae (palm family)

This often-encountered and attractive small ornamental palm has been planted in yards, parks and along streets in the V.I. and south Florida. Native to the Philippines, Christmas palm has become naturalized in the V.I., south Florida, and other tropical areas. In form, it resembles a miniature version of the Puerto Rican royal palm. It is identified by its (1) single gray trunk, with rings (leaf scars), topped by a green crown shaft; (2) rounded crown of pinnately compound leaves, the newest of which appears as a terminal spike as with royal palm; (3) a collar composed of long clusters of small gray-green to yellowish flower buds and flowers; and (4) green or red olive-shaped fruits, depending on time of year. The green and red fruits are seen together around Christmas, giving the tree its common name.

Christmas palm at the St. George Village Botanical Garden, St. Croix, in November. This specimen was 21 ft. (6.4 m) tall and 6 in. (15 cm) in dbh.

Lichen-covered bark.

Form. Christmas palm has a manicured appearance. It is usually fairly erect. It can reach 20–30 ft. (6–9 m) in height and trunk diameters of 8–10 in. (20–25 cm), but is usually smaller. The base of the trunk is slightly swollen.

Leaves and bark. The crown has about 12 leaves, each about 5 ft. (1.5 m) long, with smooth-margined leaflets about 24 in. (61 cm) long and 2 in. (5 cm) wide. The leaflets are crowded on the midribs, giving the crown a full, rich look. The bark is smooth except for the leaf scar rings.

Flowers, which appear in spring and summer, are small and inconspicuous individually but showy in their large clusters. Each flower is about 0.5 in. (1.3 cm) across, dominated by stamens. Flowers contain both male and female parts.

Fruits are about 1 in. (2.5 cm) long and 0.5 in. (1.3 cm) wide, fleshy, with a single seed. The mature red fruits can be seen at least through January.

Habitat. *Veitchia merrillii* grows in partial shade or full sun in a variety of soil types, providing they are well drained. It is moderately drought- and salt-tolerant, and shows good wind-resistance.

Uses. In the American tropics, Christmas palm has a history only as an ornamental. A viral disease called lethal yellowing limits its use in south Florida. Although several articles made reference to its use in Asia in folk medicine, no specific examples were found.

Cluster of buds with a few flowers; inset shows flower detail. The cluster was about 15 in. (38 cm) long, and the flowers 0.5 in. (1.3 cm) across.

Clusters of red and green fruit, in February on St. Croix; inset shows mature fruits, photographed in January, after many had fallen. Fruits were approximately 1.5 in. (3.8 cm) long.

Glossary

As mentioned, this book is as nearly nontechnical as I could make it. Even so, a few terms make descriptions much easier.

BOLE: The trunk below the first major branch.

BRANCH: Secondary woody stem growing off the trunk. Branches also usually have branches.

DBH: Diameter breast high (4.5 ft., 1.4 m) is a measure of trunk size used by professional foresters. It is used where possible in this book, but many trees branch near the ground, making it impossible; in such cases, I have simply described the height at which I measured the diameter.

LEAF: The photosynthesizing organs of the tree, attached to a twig or branch, and periodically shed. Leaves can be simple or compound (see description of leaf types in Introduction).

LEAFLET: A single division of a compound leaf.

LENTICEL: A corky area on the bark surfaces of twigs, branches, and sometimes trunks; they allow the exchange of gases.

MIDRIB: A compound leaf's central rib, off of which leaflets arise. Sometimes there are secondary or even tertiary midribs.

PETAL: Usually the colored, showy part of a flower, surrounding the reproductive organs; petals are separated, lobed, or tubular.

PETIOLE: The stalk of a leaf that attaches to the stem. The midrib is an extension of the petiole.

STAMEN: The filament that supports the male, pollen-producing structure; often stamens extend some distance out of the flower and can be the showiest part.

STEM: Often used interchangeably with trunk and branch.

TREE: A woody perennial plant, usually with a single main trunk, and which can reach or exceed 20 ft. (6 m) in height.

TRUNK: The main stem of the tree.

TWIG: The last subdivision of a branch; the youngest woody structure, not shed.

Sources of Information Used in Preparing this Book

In addition to the publications cited below, I made extensive use of the Internet, particularly sites by governments and universities. Among the most useful web sites were those connected with the University of Florida, Purdue University, and the U.S. Forest Service. One needs only to search under the scientific names of the trees to encounter these and many other rich sources of information.

My principal references in the following list are marked with an asterisk.

*Acevedo-Rodríguez, P. *Flora of St. John, U.S. Virgin Islands.* Memoirs of The New York Botanical Garden, Vol. 78. Bronx, New York: The New York Botanical Garden, 1996.

Ayensu, E.S. *Medicinal Plants of the West Indies.* Algonac, Michigan: Reference Publications, 1981.

*Barwick, M. *Tropical and Subtropical Trees. An Encyclopedia.* Portland, Oregon: Timber Press, 2004.

Britton, N.L., and P. Wilson. "Scientific Survey of Porto Rico and the Virgin Islands." Vols. V and VI. *Botany of Porto Rico and the Virgin Islands.* Bronx, New York: New York Academy of Sciences, 1923–1930.

*Burch, D., D.B. Ward, and D.W. Hall. *Checklist of the Woody Cultivated Plants of Florida.* Extension Sale Publication SP-33. Gainesville, Florida: Institute of Food and Agricultural Sciences, University of Florida, 1988.

Flynn, J.H., and C.D. Holder, eds. *A Guide to Useful Woods of the World.* Madison, Wisconsin: Forest Products Society, 2001.

*Gibney, E.A. *Field Guide to Native Trees and Plants of East End, St. John, U.S. Virgin Islands.* St. John, U.S. Virgin Islands: Center for the Environment, 2004.

Hammer, Roger L. *Florida Keys Wildflowers. A Field Guide to Wildflowers, Trees, Shrubs, and Woody Vines of the Florida Keys.* Guildford, Connecticut: The Globe Pequot Press, 2004.

Jones, K.D. *Native Trees for Community Forests: A Guide to Landscaping with the Native Trees of St. Croix, U.S. Virgin Islands.* Virgin Islands Department of Agriculture. St. Croix, U.S. Virgin Islands: St. George Village Botanical Garden, Inc., 1995.

Kingsbury, J. M. 200 Conspicuous, Unusual, or Economically Important Tropical Plants of the Caribbean. Ithaca, New York: Bullbrier Press, 1998.

*Little, E.L. Jr. *Atlas of United States Trees.* Vol. 5. Florida. U.S. Department of Agriculture, Forest Service. Misc. Pub. 1361, Washington, DC: Government Printing Office, 1978.

*Little, E.L. Jr., and F.H. Wadsworth. *Common Trees of Puerto Rico and the Virgin Islands.* U.S. Department of Agriculture Agricultural Handbook 249. Washington, DC: Government Printing Office, 1964.

*Little, E. L. Jr., R.O. Woodbury, and F.H. Wadsworth. *Trees of Puerto Rico and the Virgin Islands.* Second Volume. U.S. Department of Agriculture Agricultural Handbook 449. Washington, DC: Government Printing Office, 1974.

Nelson, G. *The Trees of Florida. A Reference and Field Guide.* Sarasota, Florida: Pineapple Press, 1994.

Nicholls, Robert W. *Remarkable Big Trees in the U.S. Virgin Islands.* St. Thomas: University of the Virgin Islands, 2006.

Seddon, S.A., and G.W. Lennox. *Trees of the Caribbean.* London: Macmillan, 1980.

Stebbins, M.K. *Flowering Trees of Florida.* Sarasota, Florida: Pineapple Press, 1999.

Thomas, T. *Traditional Medicinal Plants of St. Croix, St. Thomas and St. John: A Selection of 68 Plants.* St. Thomas: University of the Virgin Islands Press, 1997.

Timyan, J. Bwa Yo. *Important Trees of Haiti.* Washington, D.C., South-East Consortium for International Development, 1996.

Whistler, W.A. *Tropical Ornamentals: A Guide.* Portland, Oregon: Timber Press, 2000.

Index of Common and Latin Names

208